To Mark & Lisa,

MORE *from*

MACRINA

Celebrate the
Table!

Leslie Mackie

MORE *from* MACRINA

New Favorites from Seattle's Popular Neighborhood Bakery

LESLIE MACKIE *with* Lisa Gordanier

PHOTOGRAPHY *by* JIM HENKENS

SASQUATCH BOOKS
SEATTLE

Printed in China

Published by Sasquatch Books
17 16 15 14 13 12   9 8 7 6 5 4 3 2 1

Cover and interior photographs: Jim Henkens

Art direction and design: Anna Goldstein

Library of Congress Cataloging-in-Publication Data is available.

ISBN-13: 978-1-57061-779-9

Sasquatch Books
1904 Third Avenue, Suite 710
Seattle, WA 98101
(206) 467-4300
www.sasquatchbooks.com
custserv@sasquatchbooks.com

CONTENTS

RECIPE LIST

To Matt, Scott, Pat, and Pat

ACKNOWLEDGMENTS

It was Matt Galvin, one of our Macrina partners, who first approached me with the idea of writing another cookbook, capturing the culture and the exciting new recipes that have come about over the years of our partnership. With a slight lull in my schedule and a big desire to share our story, I jumped at the opportunity.

Heartfelt thanks to my collaborator, Lisa Gordanier. We had the pleasure of traveling to Hightower vineyard together, cooking together for our annual "Feast of Macrina" party, and spending hours volleying documents back and forth, composing the contents of this book! Thank you for your attention to detail, your great ability to translate a thought into words, and for always asking the right question to better bring out a more vivid description.

Sasquatch Books, our publishing company, is a gem with talented book visionaries, editors, designers—all adding their insight to bring the best out in their books. Gary Luke, Susan Roxborough, Rachelle Longé, Anna Goldstein, and Diane Sepanski: Thank you for all your great contributions to make this book the gorgeous collection of recipes and stories that it is.

Jim Henkens, our photographer, is a spectacular one-man show. He travels with his collection of props, camera, and laptop. Behold the brilliant images throughout this book. Anna Goldstein (our book designer) and Jim worked closely together to visually tell Macrina's story with wonderful results.

Lastly, my gratitude goes out to my partners, all our staff, and our customers, all of whom have contributed to making Macrina the thriving, forward-thinking business it is. It started as my baby and has grown with the creative and intellectual talents of so many over the past twenty years. It is with great pleasure I share the Macrina story!

—*Leslie Mackie*

There is no baking professional in Seattle I admire more than Leslie Mackie; it has been an honor and a genuine pleasure to assist her in writing this book. Leslie packs more into a day than most of us do in a week—you can't be around her for long and not catch that wave of enthusiasm and "anything's possible" attitude. With Leslie at the helm, Macrina is much more than a thriving artisan bakery—it's a company that creates partners with many individuals, organizations, and other businesses to help build a vibrant local community.

I'm very grateful to the superlative editorial and design teams at Sasquatch Books for bringing this beautiful book into reality. Last, to my mom: thank you, Edna Rose Ramseier, for instilling in me a deep respect for food. Your thoughtful, natural ability to put a meal on the table that has the perfect balance of colors, textures, and flavors has steered me well all these years.

—*Lisa Gordanier*

INTRODUCTION

Macrina Bakery opened in 1993 in a Seattle neighborhood called Belltown. Located near the ever-popular Pike Place Market, the neighborhood had seen better days—but it was revitalizing itself and seemed full of opportunity. Our original bakery was all of 847 square feet, of which two-thirds was "back of the house" for bread and pastry production. Each morning, a fellow baker and I braved the 5 a.m. hour to begin loading preformed artisan breads into our hearth oven. Another baker kept our small glass case full of fresh breakfast pastries for our hungry morning customers. An old galvanized steel baker's rack was prominently placed, full of crackling bread (the sound just-baked loaves make as they cool) fresh from the oven, replenished all day long. Those were the early days of Macrina.

❧ ❧ ❧ ❧ ❧

Fortunately the hard work paid off. The neighborhood loved having its own artisan bakery. Through our floor-to-ceiling sidewalk windows, people could watch us at all hours pulling warm loaves out of the hearth oven, or assembling cakes, forming scones, and garnishing fresh fruit tarts. In 1994 we took over a space that adjoined the bakery and excitedly opened our café. Now customers could sit down and relax with a cup of coffee and a fresh-baked pastry or warm slice of quiche. They started asking for lunch, dinner, and brunch service. Well, of course we could do that! (I have a hard time saying no.) What a great way to introduce new breads and use house favorites in sandwiches or as croutons or French toast. The café was bursting with customers.

Leslie Mackie's Macrina Bakery & Cafe Cookbook, published in 2003, was written as a tribute to our first ten years. I wanted to capture the magic of our busy little bakery—to share stories and inspirations, and to thank the very talented and hardworking staff we knew as the Macrina family.

We shared great highs, as well as weathering the growth spurts that tested our collective graciousness. Over the next year, three key managers left to pursue new opportunities; this gave me a chance to restructure job descriptions to better support the growth we were experiencing within the company.

I spent a week on awe-inspiring Vashon Island in Puget Sound (my favorite place on earth) pouring out any and all ideas about how I might capture Macrina's momentum and expand the company—gracefully and intelligently. With a dream of building one space that held both our central kitchen and our administrative offices, the answer soon became clear: I needed to find a managing partner who shared my values and work ethic, and who loved Macrina.

With the encouragement of a friend, I called Matt Galvin, one of three owners at Seattle's Pagliacci Pizza. For years I had admired Pagliacci's community presence, its customer service (like no other), and—no small thing—the authentic,

seasonal, and delicious foods it served. I left a message, introducing myself and wondering if he'd ever imagined being involved in a successful artisan bakery. Matt and his partners at Pagliacci spent the next nine months getting to know Macrina: deciding if our values, company vision, and goals lined up. In 2007, at our annual "Feast of Macrina," we formed a business partnership that would steer the bakery toward realizing its full potential.

During our first year as partners, our primary goal was to consolidate all the wholesale baking and food preparation operations into my dream central kitchen. We needed a location that was affordable but still had retail potential for a café, once again featuring those big glass windows that allow customers to view our bakers and pastry team at work. Matt stumbled upon what would become our new facility, located in the industrial but up-and-coming SoDo neighborhood. All our partners—Scott France, Matt Galvin, Pat McDonald, and Pat McCarthy—were involved, along with me, in the visualization of our new 9,000-square-foot building.

Our priorities were to build the structure in keeping with our key business principles of buying local products, using local services, and making environmentally responsible choices each step of the way. Ultimately we chose to construct our new bakery according to Leadership in Energy and Environmental Design (LEED) guidelines (an internationally recognized "green" building certification). Richard Floisand, our architect, helped put our principles into action: We laid out each department with flow and function in mind. We contracted with local crafts- and tradespeople for metalwork, display cases, lighting, furniture, and art. We added windows to bring in natural light and installed energy-efficient fixtures and appliances. When complete, our production facility earned the LEED Silver certification; to our knowledge, we were only the second baking facility in the nation to achieve this. My partners deserve the credit for making this dream a reality.

This book is titled *More from Macrina* for a reason: the name represents all that's transpired in recent years. It's filled, of course, with more Macrina favorites: breads, tempting breakfast pastries, and lots of great cookie recipes. We've developed new takes on our cherished pies and cakes. And you'll find two chapters on savory foods: brunch ideas and additional ways to use our breads. All of which take advantage of delicious seasonal ingredients and local products.

Besides the recipes, you'll find stories about some of the people and businesses who play a part in Macrina's world. We've reaped big rewards by investing in—and learning from—our talented staff. And the business partnerships we've formed over the years inspire us to do our best, knowing the integral part our products and services play in helping them succeed.

Throughout all these changes, I've gained new perspectives. Having partners with brilliant expertise and experience has allowed me to step back from business operations and, once again, work closely with our production staff. I'm in the Macrina kitchen much more often, developing new products and researching market trends. In other words, I've returned to the role that inspired me to open Macrina originally.

Gathering people to enjoy delicious food—made simply and with integrity—is something very close to my heart. I've always loved eating at home and experiencing the synergy around the table—be it a heated discussion amid a lively crowd or a quiet conversation with one other person. I hope this book will inspire you to bring friends and family to your table—and that you'll greatly enjoy preparing the recipes from this collection of our favorites. I'm certainly not the first person to say this, but I feel it from my core: gathering with others to experience a delicious meal and share stories feeds not only your body, but also your soul.

KITCHEN MUST-HAVES

Baker's Peel: A wooden paddle with a short handle that is very helpful for sliding bread onto a preheated baking stone; available at most specialty cooking stores in wood or a dishwasher-safe composite material. If you don't have a baker's peel, use a piece of parchment paper laid on top of an upside-down baking sheet; place the loaves or rolls on the parchment for their final rise, then slide them, paper and all, onto the preheated stone.

Baking Stone: A good baking stone is one of your most important tools for baking artisan breads and pizza crusts. Preheated in a very hot oven, the stone creates the best surface to give the loaf its "oven spring" (adding height and volume to your final product). It also encourages a deep brown, crisp crust. Look for a 14-by-16-inch ceramic pizza stone. A newer product is the Emile Henry grilling stone; it's made of a specially glazed ceramic material that cleans up easily and won't retain oil spots.

Bamboo Skewers: Used for testing the doneness of cakes and muffins; available in specialty cooking stores and many grocery stores.

Bench Knife: A key baker's tool, the bench knife is a 6-by-4½-inch rectangular metal plate with a slightly sharpened edge on one side and a wood or plastic handle on the other. It's perfect for cutting and dividing bread, scone, and biscuit doughs; for straightening the sides of scones and cakes; and for scraping your work surface clean of floury residue. It also comes in a plastic version that is somewhat flexible, which is great for scraping bowls—plus, it won't scratch your work surface. Both are very useful and quite inexpensive; I'd recommend getting one of each.

Cake Pans: Heavier, commercial-grade cake pans bake the most evenly. Chicago Metallic makes a nice "Commercial II" 9-inch straight-sided cake pan, found in specialty cooking stores. It comes in either a 2-inch- or 3-inch-tall version; I prefer the taller one. You can choose pans with either a removable or a fixed bottom; one advantage of the former is that you can use the flat, thin bottom piece as a base on which to assemble a cake. It's also very helpful for lifting cake layers and placing them precisely where you want them.

Citrus Juicer: There's no good substitute for fresh lemon, lime, or orange juice. You can still find the old-fashioned cone-shaped strainers that fit over a cup, but somewhat newer on the market are hand-held juicers that squeeze the halved fruit between two hinged levers. BergHOFF makes a good metal version (generally superior to plastic versions, which tend to flex too much for effective juicing).

Cupcake/Muffin Baking Pans: Again, heavier pans always bake better. I like Chicago Metallic's 12-cup muffin pans, found in specialty cooking stores.

The company also makes a jumbo-size pan (perfect for Almond Cake with Raspberries and Chocolate Ganache, page 155) and a 24-cup mini-muffin pan, great for smaller cupcakes or breakfast buffet muffins.

Cupcake/Muffin Liners: You can purchase decorative papers with colorful designs in specialty cooking stores, while plain-colored liners are easily found in your local supermarket. "Jumbo" refers to oversize papers; both "standard" and "large" designations are used for standard-size muffins or cupcakes. I look for the "If You Care" brand: they are unbleached, nonstick, and compostable.

Food Processor: A convenience that has become standard equipment in many kitchens. Great for grinding nuts, making purees, and mixing some doughs. Choose a brand based on performance (Cuisinart still sets the standard for home food processors) and a model based on its capacity (bowl size) and horsepower. For example, a 4-cup "mini-prep" processor is fine for grinding small amounts of nuts or bread crumbs, or pureeing fruit. A more versatile machine can hold between 7 and 14 cups, allowing you to do a wider variety of tasks. KitchenAid now makes a 12-cup model that has three interchangeable bowls to accommodate both small and large jobs.

Kitchen Towels: I keep a supply of clean kitchen towels for proofing bread (letting the dough rise). The best I've found is the lint-free Ritz Royale Wonder Towel designed for cleaning glasses. Widely available and inexpensive cotton flour-sack towels work well too. Just look for non–terry cloth, lint-free towels.

Knives: An 8- or 10-inch chef's knife, a serrated knife (sometimes just called a bread knife), and a paring knife are the essential three. LamsonSharp, Wüsthof, and Henckels are all excellent choices. It's best to go to a store and hold the knives in your hand, checking for size, weight, balance, and comfort. Carbon steel blades hold the best edge.

Measuring Cups and Spoons: Sturdy metal cups will last the longest. The new kid on the block is the Chef'n Pinch+Pour collapsible measuring cup—great for a culinary student's tool kit or an overcrowded kitchen drawer because of its compact size.

Microplane: This grating tool has become a kitchen standard for good reason: it's perfect for zesting citrus peel and for finely grating cheese.

Offset Spatulas: Inexpensive and ergonomic, these spatulas are a must for baking and frosting cakes. Their offset design makes it easier to apply even pressure to the frosting, thus giving you straighter, smoother surfaces. Get at least two sizes: a 4-inch blade for cupcakes and narrow pans, and a 7-inch blade for everything else.

Parchment Paper: Many of the recipes in this book call for a parchment paper–lined baking sheet. I simply cut the paper to the size of my sheet and fold any edges under if needed. Rolls of parchment are available at most grocery stores; precut rounds (to aid in releasing cake layers from pans) are available in specialty cooking stores.

Pastry Brushes: These days, silicone pastry brushes are all the rage. I prefer to use natural bristle brushes, though silicone brushes have two advantages: they don't shed, and you can clean them easily in your dishwasher. Whichever you choose, have a few different sizes for brushing flour off your work surface, applying egg wash to delicate pastries, and so on.

Rimmed Baking Sheets: Chicago Metallic makes great commercial-grade jelly-roll pans measuring 16¾ by 12 by 1 inch. They're really just heavy-duty baking sheets. Buy at least two—they'll last a lifetime—then toss out all those old flimsy, warped cookie sheets!

Rolling Pins: I like the wooden 12-by-2¾-inch rolling pins with handles, but many bakers prefer a dowel-type (aka French) 2-inch rolling pin. Both styles are great. Wipe down and dry them well after each use to prevent swelling.

Rubber Spatulas: The classic Rubbermaid spatula—now made in a high-heat version—is one of my most-used kitchen tools. Alternatively, many flexible spatulas are now made of silicone; they also withstand very high heats and are extremely durable. To jazz up your kitchen, they come in all colors, designs, and shapes.

Scoops: Various brands and sizes of ice cream–type scoops are available in specialty cooking stores. OXO Good Grips scoops, for example, come in large, medium, and small sizes. In this book we often refer to the #30 scoop (found in restaurant supply stores), which is roughly equivalent to the medium scoop listed above. I use them for a variety of kitchen chores, from scooping batter into muffin pans to portioning cookies, dolloping frostings and fillings, and making meatballs.

Sifter: Most pastry recipes require some sifting. I use a handheld 8-inch strainer to do the job. It rests on the rim of a bowl or can be tapped against your other hand to pass the ingredients through the mesh.

Spray Bottle: Home bread bakers should mist the inside of their ovens with a standard plastic spray bottle filled with water; it will create a humid environment right at the beginning of baking. (Commercial bread ovens have built-in steam injectors for just this purpose.) The moist steam allows the dough to expand freely before it forms a crust and sets, so the loaf can rise to its fullest potential. Additionally, surface moisture contributes to the beautiful browning of the crust.

Stand Mixer: A kitchen tool you *really* must have. If you make bread, a heavy-duty model will perform best and last longest; for pastry and small recipes, a less expensive model works great. KitchenAid made the modern stand mixer what it is today, and its products are widely available in several sizes and in many fun colors. Truly a well-designed kitchen convenience!

Wire Cooling Rack: Proper cooling is important to the overall success of your baked goods. A sturdy wire mesh rack—one with wires running both ways in a grid design—offers more support than one with the wires running just the length of the rack. In addition, those one-way wires can create deep grooves in the soft surfaces of your baked items.

KITCHEN NICE-TO-HAVES

Cake Decorating Turntable: A cake turntable is basically a cake stand on a pedestal that elevates and spins a cake while you assemble and decorate it. The beauty is that the turntable supports the cake so you can steady your body, hands, and tools—resulting in a much more professional-looking finished product. Ateco makes one with a sturdy cast-iron base and an aluminum turntable top; it's the one most professionals use. There are also plastic versions, usually with shorter pedestals, that work fine but may be less durable.

Cake Knife: An extra-long (12 or 15 inches) serrated knife for cutting evenly through cake layers.

Cellophane Bags: These clear plastic bags come in a variety of sizes for decorative gift giving. I like to have them on hand to package cookies and other sweets.

Decorative Plates: You'll love having even a few special presentation plates for your baked creations. They should have a 10-inch-diameter flat center, with the rim extending beyond that. Easily picked up at secondhand stores, they're also lovely to get or give as hostess gifts.

Double Dutch Oven: For breads that are baked inside a cast-iron dutch oven, like those in our Artisanal Breads chapter, this is the one you want. It has a flat lid (as opposed to typical dutch oven, which has a looped handle on the lid) that can double as an inverted flat griddle. Lodge makes a great version. (See Dutch Ovens, page 44, for more information.)

Food Scale: A scale (most are electronic now) allows you to accurately measure wet or dry ingredients and evenly divide dough and batters. For recipes that benefit from precise measurements—like most baked goods—using a scale is faster, more precise, and less messy than measuring in cups.

Glass Pie Plates: If you're spending precious time to bake a pie, why not present it in a beautiful dish? I prefer the way glass and ceramic plates bake a pie (as compared to metal or disposable aluminum pans). Pyrex pans are by far the most commonly used, and they do a great job. For variety, collect Emile Henry pie plates or even those made by your local glass artists.

Herb Garden: I encourage everyone to have window planters, balcony boxes, or garden areas for fresh herbs and edible flowers. They're so easy to grow and will reward you tenfold for your efforts. Using fresh herbs takes your food to another level of interest, adding fresh yet complex flavors—and they make beautiful garnishes as well. Edible flowers such as nasturtiums, Johnny-jump-ups, roses, and calendulas are wonderful on cakes, appetizer platters, and in salads.

Spice Grinder: A small electric coffee grinder works great for spices; I keep a separate grinder for spices only. Whole spices retain more flavor and can be ground in seconds.

Waffle Iron: Great to have for leisurely weekend breakfasts. There are some that fit on top of your burners and then flip to cook the waffles on both sides. Of course, there are many electric waffle irons too; Chef's Choice makes a nice one called the "Belgian WafflePro."

INGREDIENTS

Canola Oil: I use canola oil for greasing cake pans, muffin pans, and cookie sheets because it has a high burning point and imparts little flavor.

Chocolate: Chocolate for baking and eating comes in varying levels of sweetness. Simple distinctions are as follows: unsweetened chocolate contains 100 percent cocoa solids (used for baking only); bittersweet averages from 62 to 80 percent cocoa solids; and semisweet typically ranges from 35 to 60 percent cocoa solids. The higher the percentage of cocoa solids, the more intense the chocolate flavor and the lower the sugar level. There are many chocolate producers now, and you can get as local or exotic as you like. One good guideline is to cook with a chocolate that you enjoy eating. Ghirardelli and Callebaut are good-quality, readily available brands.

Cocoa Powder: All our recipes use Dutch-process cocoa powder because we prefer its flavor and performance. Cocoa powder is the dried chocolate liquor left behind after the cocoa butter has been removed from the fermented, dried, and roasted cocoa nibs. The unsweetened chocolate liquor is treated with an alkaline (low-acid) solution to neutralize its acidity; this process removes the harshness and bitterness, leaving a darker-colored and more intensely chocolate-flavored powder. If you'd like to substitute natural cocoa powder for Dutch-process, consult a reliable baking book for guidelines.

Edible Flowers: Of course, it's best (and by far the most fun!) to garnish your baked goods with flowers from your garden or window box. But if you buy them from a florist, check to make sure they're pesticide-free. At the very least, always wash them in water and air-dry.

Eggs: I buy local, cage-free eggs with no growth hormones—organic whenever possible. The nutritional quality of eggs declines with age, so check the pull date and choose the freshest ones.

Egg Substitutes: For vegan diets, it's necessary to replace the eggs in baked goods with other ingredients. There are various egg substitutes on the market, some better for baking than others. These products will add some richness and leavening power to the final product. You can now find egg replacements in the baking section at most grocery stores. We use the potato and tapioca starch–based Ener-G Egg Replacer.

Egg Whites: If you use egg whites that aren't going to be cooked, it's best to buy them pasteurized (look for them in your supermarket's dairy section).

Flour: Most of the recipes in this book call for unbleached all-purpose flour; Stone-Buhr's Shepherd's Grain Flour is my favorite. For specialty flours such as rye, whole wheat, corn, and gluten-free alternatives, I always try to buy whole grain milled flours (see Whole Grain Milling: A Revolution in the Right Direction, page 48). They may be more expensive, but they're more nutritious and have superior flavor. If you can't find them in your grocery store's baking section, look online. I purchase small bags and store them in airtight containers in a cool, dry place to maintain freshness.

Nuts: I recommend buying whole raw nuts, then toasting and chopping them as needed (see Toasting Tips, page 7, for more information). Prepackaged nuts tend to be less fresh and more expensive, so I always buy nuts from my supermarket's bulk section.

Olive Oils: Olive oils are really the best all-purpose oil for savory dishes. I use both pure and extra-virgin olive oils in my recipes. Pure olive oil is a blend of a lower-grade, more refined oil with virgin oil. It's cheaper and more suitable for recipes that call for a neutral-flavored oil. It also has a higher smoke point than extra-virgin, so it's preferable for sautéing. Extra-virgin olive oils have a lot of complex flavors that add to the overall flavor of a dish. These vary widely, so if it's possible, taste before you buy.

Vegan Butter: A butter substitute made of expeller-pressed natural oils such as soybean, palm, canola, and olive. I often use the Earth Balance brand; note that it's salted, so take this into consideration when baking with it. You can now find vegan butter at Whole Foods and most natural food stores.

Vegan Sugar: Beet sugar is probably the most widely used vegan sugar; it's acceptable to those on a vegan diet because it's not filtered using charred animal bone meal, as processed sugar made from sugar cane is. Another option is turbinado sugar, which is raw cane sugar manufactured in a way that doesn't use bone char.

Vegetable Oil Sprays: These are convenience products used for spraying pans so that your baked goods won't stick. They're pretty handy and work especially well for pans with lots of nooks and crannies, like Bundt pans and waffle irons.

Xanthan Gum: Made from fermented corn syrup, xanthan gum binds and adds volume to gluten-free baked products such as breads, biscuits, cakes, and cookies. Without its addition, these items would be quite crumbly and wouldn't hold their shape, so don't be tempted to leave it out, even though the amounts you use are quite small.

BREADS
& ROLLS

Vollkorn Bread 5

Fresh Herb Baguette 9

SoDo Rolls 12

Pretzel Knot Rolls 14

THE TERM "BREADHEAD" is commonly used to describe people who, before taking a bite of sourdough, first lift it to their noses and inhale deeply; or who examine the interior cell structure of a loaf of *levain* (and are compelled to comment on it to anyone who happens to be within earshot); or who ogle a baguette's bronzed crust, marveling at the range of colors produced by the process of caramelization. Additional breadhead characteristics may be planning a vacation that focuses on hitting all the bakeries and mills in the state of Vermont (with perhaps a *little* sightseeing on the side), or going to France for a hands-on baking class at the venerable Ecole Française de Boulangerie and Patisserie d'Aurillac. Isn't it amazing how four simple ingredients can capture our attention and produce such flavorful, soul-satisfying results? Go ahead and admit it: You too are a breadhead!

The heartbeat of Macrina has always been bread—it's why I founded Macrina Bakery way back in 1993. Our first cookbook included many of our customers' favorites, some European and some American in style. They tended to be on the equipment- and labor-intensive side—so for this book, I've selected recipes that retain the best of the artisan bread spirit but fit better into our busy lives.

Starters, seed doughs, and soakers are prepared the night before (beginning the process of fermentation while you sleep), bringing fantastic flavor to the finished loaf. Simple steps such as toasting grains, choosing locally milled whole grain flours, and using fresh-picked garden herbs also bring out sparks of flavor and add depth.

Several of these flavor-enhancing steps are put into use in our ever-popular Vollkorn Bread, made with a trio of earthy, whole grain flours. SoDo Rolls are unbeatable for a barbecue—they offer a great alternative to those puffy store-bought buns. For world-class sandwiches, try the Pretzel Knot Rolls, made with rye flour and brushed with a baking soda wash to get that classic burnished mahogany finish. Or get down and floury with our Fresh Herb Baguette, made with vibrant garden herbs and topped with the crunchy tang of sea salt.

Whether you enjoy the baking or the breaking of bread, you'll find these varieties delicious, versatile, and fun to make! After twenty-five years of having bread as my passion, I'm proud to be called a breadhead.

Vollkorn Bread

This German-style whole grain bread has been a favorite from the first time we proudly placed it on our bread racks. Originally we used a natural sourdough starter made with hops from a friend's beer-making project! The sour starter contrasts with the sweetness of the honey and agave syrup, giving a satisfying dimension of flavor not found in many whole grain breads. In adapting this recipe for the home baker, I've created a "soaker" made with medium-bodied beer, which ensures a full-flavored and very moist final loaf.

MAKES ONE 12-INCH BRAIDED LOAF

1. Make the soaker the night before to hydrate the four-grain cereal and begin developing the dough's complex flavors. Our cereal mix includes whole cracked wheat, organic steel-cut oats, whole rye grits, and whole barley grits, but you can create your own combination or check your supermarket's bulk foods section for premixed combinations.

2. Preheat the oven to 350°F. Spread the cereal on a rimmed baking sheet and toast for 10 minutes, or until it has browned slightly. Pour the cereal into a medium bowl. Add the flax seeds, flour, and beer, and whisk until no lumps remain. Cover the bowl loosely with plastic wrap and let it sit at room temperature for at least 10 hours.

3. To make the dough, lightly oil a medium bowl with canola oil and line a rimmed baking sheet with parchment paper. Set aside. Fill a spray bottle with water and set aside.

4. In the bowl of a stand mixer fitted with the paddle attachment, mix the soaker, yeast, filtered water, agave syrup, and honey on low speed for 2 minutes. (Or mix by hand, placing the ingredients in a large bowl and whisking to combine.) Add the flours, pumpkin and sunflower seeds (reserving 2 tablespoons of the pumpkin seeds and 1 tablespoon of the sunflower seeds to use as garnish), and kosher salt.

5. Switch to the dough hook and mix on the lowest speed for 10 minutes. The dough will ball at the base of the hook. (If mixing by hand, stir with a wooden spoon or rubber spatula until the dough comes together. Transfer the dough to a floured work surface and knead for 10 minutes.) Transfer the dough to the prepared bowl and cover with plastic wrap. Set the dough in a warm place (about 75°F) and let it rise

FOR THE SOAKER:

⅓ cup four-grain cereal

1 tablespoon flax seeds

½ cup (2¼ ounces) stone-ground whole wheat flour

¾ cup (6 ounces) amber beer

FOR THE BREAD DOUGH:

Soaker, at room temperature

1 teaspoon active dry yeast

⅔ cup filtered water

1 tablespoon amber agave syrup

2 tablespoons honey

¾ cup (3½ ounces) unbleached all-purpose flour

¾ cup (3½ ounces) stone-ground whole wheat flour

½ cup (2 ounces) stone-ground rye flour

¼ cup plus 1 tablespoon raw pumpkin seeds, toasted (see Toasting Tips, page 7) and coarsely chopped, divided

¼ cup raw sunflower seeds, toasted and chopped, divided

1 tablespoon kosher salt

1 large egg beaten with 1 tablespoon water, for egg wash

1 teaspoon coarse sea salt, for garnish

for 2 hours. (Because this is a fairly heavy dough, it will rise but not double in size.)

6. Transfer the dough from the bowl onto a floured work surface and punch it down with your hands. Using a bench knife or a plastic dough scraper, divide the dough into thirds. Roll out each piece into a 10-inch-long rope. Line up three strands side by side and, starting at one end, weave them into a braid. Be careful not to weave them too tightly because the bread must be able to expand as it rises and bakes. Pinch the ends together to form a seal, then tuck them under. Using the palms of your hands to create a rocking motion over these ends will create a desirable tapered look.

7. Place the loaf on the prepared baking sheet and cover with plastic wrap. Let the dough proof (rise) for about 1 hour.

8. About 20 minutes before baking, position a rack in the center of the oven and preheat to 375°F.

9. Brush the loaf lightly with the egg wash, then sprinkle with the reserved pumpkin and sunflower seeds and the sea salt. Using the spray bottle, heavily mist the inside of the oven with water; the steam will help the loaf expand to its fullest potential before the crust sets. Mist twice more during the first 10 minutes of baking. Bake for about 45 minutes, or until the loaf is deep brown and sounds hollow when tapped on the bottom. Cool on a wire rack for at least 30 minutes before slicing.

❈ Toasting Tips ❈

Here are some basic guidelines for toasting nuts, seeds, and coconut to crisp the ingredients and bring out an extra dimension of flavor that will make all your baked goods even more delicious.

NUTS

There's something many cooks often forget about when toasting nuts: yes, you are browning them to enhance their complex flavors, but at the same time you are *drying* them so they become wonderfully crisp. Nuts that are toasted at too high of a temperature will brown very quickly; they can end up with nearly burned exteriors but insides that are still chewy. However, if you proceed with a little patience (a lower oven temperature and a longer baking time), they'll end up perfectly toasted. Different nuts toast at different rates, depending on the variety and whether they're whole or in pieces. Walnuts, pecans, cashews, and pine nuts are quite high in fat and will toast faster than those with less oil; whole almonds and hazelnuts, which are both denser varieties, take a little longer.

To get the best results, spread the nuts in one layer on a heavy baking sheet. Bake at 300 to 325°F on the center oven rack until they are golden brown and fragrant, shaking the pan a few times for even coloring. Total baking time will be somewhere between 5 and 15 minutes; check every few minutes and definitely use your nose to alert you when they're getting close.

If you want to remove any skins after toasting, do so while the nuts are still warm. Rub them between your hands or in a clean kitchen towel to loosen the skins. Don't worry about getting every bit of skin off though—that's virtually impossible, and anyway, a little of it looks lovely and may even add a bit of flavor.

SEEDS

The same basic rules for toasting nuts apply to seeds, but you'll need to take extra care since they are so small and easy to burn. Bake pumpkin, sunflower, and sesame seeds at 300°F for 4 to 10 minutes, shaking and rotating the pan as needed. You can also toast them in a dry skillet over medium heat; shake the pan regularly and keep tossing them to avoid burning.

COCONUT

Dried coconut comes either sweetened or unsweetened, shredded or in flakes (small or large). The toasting guidelines are similar to nuts, but be absolutely sure to set the oven temperature no higher than 300°F—coconut crisps fast. Use a spoon or spatula to redistribute the pieces on the baking sheet as they brown, which should just take a few minutes.

Fresh Herb Baguette

Since long baguettes can be tricky to bake in a home oven, I've adapted this recipe so they fit nicely on a baking stone. Almost any fresh herb will taste great baked into this loaf, so choose your favorites and have fun: standouts are oregano, chives, thyme, Italian parsley, rosemary, and dill. The work is worth the prize of these fragrant, crisp loaves!

MAKES FOUR 12-INCH BAGUETTES

1. Lightly oil a medium bowl with canola oil. Line a rimmed baking sheet with a clean cotton flour-sack towel and sprinkle it heavily with flour. Set aside. Fill a spray bottle with water and set aside.

2. In the bowl of a stand mixer fitted with the paddle attachment, mix the water, yeast, and seed dough on low speed for 1 minute. (Or mix by hand, placing the ingredients in a large bowl and whisking to dissolve the yeast and break up the dough.) Let the mixture stand for 3 minutes to activate the yeast.

3. Add the olive oil, herbs, flour, and kosher salt and mix for about 2 minutes, or until the dough comes together. (If mixing by hand, use a rubber spatula to scoop the dough from the sides of the bowl, folding it into the center.) Switch to the dough hook and mix on medium speed for 12 to 14 minutes. This is a fairly wet dough. Toward the end of the mixing time you will notice that the dough develops a ball around the hook, but it will still be tethered at the base of the bowl; you'll also hear a slight slapping noise as it goes around. (If mixing my hand, once the dough has come together, transfer it to a floured work surface and knead for 12 to 14 minutes.) With floured fingers, pinch a big piece of dough and pull it away from the mass. It should stretch about 3 inches without tearing—it will feel a bit like a rubber band. If it doesn't pass this test, mix for another 1 to 3 minutes.

4. Scoop the dough out onto a floured work surface with a rubber spatula. Form the dough into a loose ball, transfer to the prepared bowl, and cover with plastic wrap. Let the dough rise at room temperature (65 to 75°F) until it has about doubled in size, about 2 hours.

5. About 20 minutes before baking, place a baking stone on the center rack of the oven and preheat to 400°F. (I can fit all 4 baguettes onto my 12-by-14-inch stone, but use a larger one if you have it.)

1 cup lukewarm filtered water (about 80°F)

1 teaspoon active dry yeast

4 ounces (½ cup) Seed Dough (page 22)

2 tablespoons extra-virgin olive oil

1 tablespoon chopped assorted fresh herbs

2½ cups plus 2 tablespoons (11½ ounces) unbleached all-purpose flour

1¼ teaspoons kosher salt

1 tablespoon coarse sea salt, for garnish

6. Transfer the dough from the bowl onto your floured work surface and flatten it into a 4-by-6-inch rectangle. Cut the rectangle in half lengthwise, then cut each long piece into 2 equal pieces. Flatten each piece with your fingertips, placing the long side in front of you. Roll it up, tucking the dough fairly tightly as you form a rope. Using the palms of both hands, roll back and forth over the top of the rope, gently extending it until it's about 12 inches long. Lift the baguettes onto the prepared towel, seam side up, spacing them at equal intervals. Pull the towel up 2 inches to form a "wall" between each baguette. (See photo, opposite. The towel acts as a mold to keep each baguette in a long, slender shape as it rises.) There's no need to cover the dough—you actually want the loaves to dry out a little so they're easier to transfer to the oven. Let the loaves rise at room temperature for 35 to 40 minutes. They should look slightly puffy but will not have risen dramatically.

7. Pull the towel out, flattening the walls between the baguettes. Gently roll the baguettes over so the dry sides are facedown. Using both hands, lift each loaf onto a baker's peel. Arrange the baguettes in a line about 2 inches apart. (If the baguettes are touching each other, they will not bake well.) Using a sharp paring knife, make four 2-inch diagonal cuts across the top of each baguette. Using the spray bottle, mist the top of each baguette and sprinkle each with a little of the sea salt.

8. Slide all 4 loaves onto the preheated baking stone. Heavily mist the inside of the oven with water; the steam will help the loaves expand to their fullest potential before the crust sets. Mist twice more during the first 10 minutes of baking. Bake for 25 to 30 minutes, or until the crust is light golden brown and the loaves sound hollow when tapped on the bottom. Cool on a wire rack for 45 minutes before slicing. These loaves are best the day they're baked.

SoDo Rolls

¾ cup lukewarm filtered water (about 80°F)

¾ cup lukewarm whole milk (about 80°F)

1½ teaspoons active dry yeast

¼ cup sugar

2 large eggs

⅓ cup pure olive oil

4¼ cups (19 ounces) unbleached all-purpose flour

2½ teaspoons kosher salt

1 large egg beaten with 1 tablespoon water, for egg wash

We opened our LEED-certified (Leadership in Energy and Environmental Design) baking facility in 2008 in Seattle's SoDo neighborhood, which gets its name from its location "south of the dome," referring to a long-gone landmark: the Kingdome sports stadium. (The Kingdome has since been replaced by not one, but two, state-of-the-art stadiums.) This roll is terrific as the foundation of a sloppy pulled-pork sandwich, a juicy hamburger, or a grilled ahi tuna sandwich. Here in Seattle, it's a tailgate party necessity.

MAKES 12 SANDWICH ROLLS

1. Lightly oil a medium bowl with canola oil and line 2 rimmed baking sheets with parchment paper. Set aside. Fill a spray bottle with water and set aside.

2. In the bowl of a stand mixer fitted with the paddle attachment, mix the filtered water, milk, yeast and sugar on low speed for 30 seconds. (Or mix by hand, placing the ingredients in a large bowl and whisking to dissolve the sugar and yeast.) Let the mixture sit for 3 minutes to activate the yeast.

3. Add the eggs and olive oil and mix for about 1 minute. Add the flour and salt, and mix on low speed for about 2 more minutes. (If mixing by hand, use a rubber spatula to scoop the dough from the sides of the bowl, folding it into the center.) Switch to the dough hook and mix on medium speed for 10 to 13 minutes. Toward the end of the mixing time you will notice that the dough develops a ball around the hook, but it will still be tethered at the base of the bowl; you'll also hear a slight slapping noise as it goes around. (If mixing my hand, once the dough has come together, transfer it to a floured work surface and knead for 10 to 13 minutes.) With floured fingers, pinch a big piece of dough and pull it away from the mass. It should stretch about 3 inches without tearing—it will feel a bit like a rubber band. If it doesn't pass this test, mix for another 1 to 3 minutes. Transfer the dough to the prepared bowl and cover with plastic wrap. Let it rise for 2 hours; it will about double in size.

4. Transfer the dough from the bowl to a floured work surface. With a bench knife or plastic dough scraper, divide the dough into twelve 3-ounce pieces. (If you don't have a scale, divide the dough by first flattening it into a rectangle about 5 by 12 inches. Divide this rectangle into 12 equal pieces: first halve it in the long direction, then cut each

half into 6 pieces in the shorter direction.) A consistent size is important so the rolls bake evenly.

5. Shape each dough piece into a ball by first flattening it and then gathering the edges toward the center. Flip the dough over so the seam side is down. Then cup the roll in the palm of your hand, keeping your fingertips and the heel of your hand resting on the work surface. Move your hand in a circular motion to tighten the surface of the roll so it will rise evenly. (You'll notice that it's important to have just a light dusting of flour on your work surface—too much and the dough will slide around; too little and it will refuse to do much besides stick to the tabletop.) Place the rolls about 2 inches apart on the prepared baking sheets. Lightly cover with plastic wrap to prevent a skin from forming on the top of the dough. Let the rolls rise at room temperature (65 to 75°F) for 1 to 1½ hours. The dough will be soft and springy to the touch (like a marshmallow) when it's ready to bake.

6. About 20 minutes before baking, position 2 racks in the center of the oven and preheat to 400°F. (Avoid the top and bottom racks; because there is sugar in the dough, the rolls will burn easily.)

7. Brush the rolls all over with the egg wash. If you miss a spot, it will show, so take your time and brush each roll completely. Using the spray bottle, heavily mist the inside of the oven with water; the steam will help the rolls expand to their fullest potential before the crusts set. Mist twice more during the first 10 minutes of baking. Bake for 20 to 25 minutes, or until the rolls are a deep golden brown. Transfer the rolls onto a wire rack by sliding them, parchment and all, from the baking sheet. After 10 minutes, remove the parchment so the rolls can cool for another 20 minutes before serving. These rolls freeze beautifully for up to 3 weeks in a resealable plastic bag, so save any extras for impromptu parties.

Pretzel Knot Rolls

1¾ cups lukewarm filtered water (about 80°F)

1½ teaspoons active dry yeast

1 tablespoon amber agave syrup

4¼ cups (19 ounces) unbleached all-purpose flour

¼ cup (1 ounce) stone-ground dark rye flour

2½ teaspoons kosher salt

1 tablespoon baking soda beaten with ¼ cup filtered water, for pretzel wash

2 tablespoons raw sesame seeds, for garnish

2 tablespoons poppy seeds, for garnish

1 tablespoon coarse sea salt, for garnish

Macrina produces about 350 different freshly baked bread and pastry items every single day. But sometimes a restaurant or customer has an inspiration for an item that's not on our current list—and this might start the wheels in motion for a new product. This pretzel roll was brought to life that way. Its bagel-like texture is enhanced with a small addition of rye flour and the roll is finished with a baking soda wash to add that characteristic pretzel flavor and deep mahogany color. It apparently struck a chord with our regulars too—it's now a very popular lunch item in our cafés.

MAKES 10 SANDWICH-SIZE ROLLS

1. Lightly oil a medium bowl with canola oil and line 2 rimmed baking sheets with parchment paper. Set aside. Fill a spray bottle with water and set aside.

2. In the bowl of a stand mixer fitted with the paddle attachment, mix the water, yeast, and agave syrup on low speed for 1 minute. (Or mix by hand, placing the ingredients in a large bowl and whisking to dissolve the yeast.) Let the mixture sit for 3 minutes to activate the yeast.

3. Add the flours and kosher salt, and mix for 1 minute. Switch to the dough hook and mix on low speed for 6 to 8 minutes, or until the dough has formed a ball at the base of the hook and has an elastic texture. (If mixing by hand, add the flours and salt, and use a wooden spoon or rubber spatula to mix until combined. Transfer the dough from the bowl onto a floured surface. Knead by hand for 6 to 8 minutes.) This is a firm dough, and it will climb up the hook as you are mixing. I stop the mixer every 2 minutes or so and pull the dough back to the base of the hook, then continue. The finished dough will be warm to the touch. Transfer the dough to the prepared bowl and cover with plastic wrap. Let it rise for 2 hours at room temperature; it will almost double in size.

4. Transfer the dough from the bowl onto a floured work surface. With a bench knife or plastic dough scraper, divide the dough into ten 4-ounce pieces. (If you don't have a scale, divide the dough by first flattening it into a rectangle about 5 by 10 inches. Cut the rectangle in half lengthwise, then cut each long piece into 5 equal pieces.) A consistent size is important so the rolls bake evenly.

5. Flatten each piece into a 2-by-4-inch rectangle. Starting with a long edge, which should be closest to you, begin rolling the dough into a rope shape. Keep rolling the rope, using the palms of your hands and rolling from the center out to the ends, until it's about 12 inches long. Loosely form it into a knot by laying the rope in a circle shape and pulling one end through the center, like a shoelace. Don't tighten the knot too much, as the rolls will rise both before baking and when they're in the oven; it's important to give them room to expand gracefully. The finished circle should be about 3 inches in diameter, with the ends extending beyond the circle about 1 inch. Place the rolls 1½ inches apart on the prepared baking sheets. Cover with plastic wrap and let the dough rise for 1 to 1½ hours; it will about double in size. The dough will be soft and springy to the touch (like a marshmallow) when it's ready to bake.

6. About 20 minutes before baking, position 2 racks in the center of the oven and preheat to 400°F.

7. Brush the pretzel wash over the rolls and garnish with the sesame and poppy seeds and the sea salt. Using the spray bottle, heavily mist the inside of the oven with water; the steam will help the rolls expand to their fullest potential before the crusts set. Mist twice more during the first 10 minutes of baking. Bake for 25 to 30 minutes, or until the rolls are a deep golden brown. Transfer the rolls onto a wire rack by sliding them, parchment and all, from the baking sheet. After 10 minutes, remove the parchment and cool for an additional 20 minutes.

❖ PHUONG HOANG BUI ❖

There are few things in life that I find as satisfying as seeing our employees gain skills, take on more responsibilities, and ultimately become stronger, more capable individuals. Phuong Hoang Bui has accomplished all this and more. Along with his significant baking and managerial skills, Phuong inspires me with his genuine good nature, his problem-solving abilities, and his desire to truly make the best of each day.

I met Phuong through the International Rescue Committee, where he was anxiously awaiting being placed in a job. Even with our limited ability to communicate, I could tell he had a great attitude and a genuine desire to work and learn, and I hired him on the spot to work as our dishwasher. That was February 1994—just six months after we'd opened Macrina.

Phuong had been trying to make his way to the United States for quite some time. His first attempt was as a boat refugee, which ended in capture and imprisonment for two years. Upon release, two fortuitous things happened: First, a fellow inmate who owned a bakery in Vietnam hired him, seeding his interest in baking. Then his mother introduced him to a friend's daughter, and they married shortly after. When he arrived in Seattle in 1993 with his wife (who had dual citizenship) and three-year-old daughter, he was welcomed with open arms to live with a local family for three months. This was such a gift to Phuong; he spoke very little English and it was a very different world from small-town life in Bien Hoa, not far from Ho Chi Minh City.

Phuong was driven by the hope of more opportunity in America. All the while dishwashing (and whistling, which he was known to do), Phuong was learning at Macrina: he'd jump in to help with food prep, watch the bakers load the ovens, and help shape bread.

Later in 1994, Macrina was fortunate to win second place in a *Sunset* magazine sourdough bread–baking contest. Business doubled almost overnight—there was no choice but to add a night shift. Phuong jumped at the opportunity to join the bakers on the night crew. And it made perfect sense: from the get-go he had an intuitive understanding about bread baking—something that can't always be taught. Within a few years, Phuong was promoted to lead night baker, and in 2001 he took on the demanding job of overseeing both the day and night shifts.

To date, Phuong has worked at Macrina for eighteen years. He now manages the entire wholesale production team: about fifty bakery and pastry employees. Phuong's staff is diverse in age and ethnicity: many are newly arrived from Vietnam and very few have baking experience. He understands how difficult it is to begin a new life in America, and by helping his staff learn and adjust to life in Seattle, he hopes to repay the kindness he was shown when he arrived almost twenty years ago.

Now I watch Phuong shaping bread alongside his crew, speeding production along and confidently discussing challenges with purveyors and maintenance staff. I hear him talk with pride about his grown daughter. I recognized Phuong's potential early on, but his accomplishments stand alone.

ITALIAN BREADS & FLATBREADS

AS A STUDENT AT THE California Culinary Academy, I learned the simple differences between French and Italian cooking this way: a favorite chef-instructor, Carlo Middione, demonstrated how a breast of chicken cooked Italian-style would be left bone-in, marinated with the simplest ingredients, then roasted in a wood-burning oven for the truest overall flavor. For the French preparation, he deboned and butterflied the chicken breast, then sautéed it in a hot pan, flambéed it with brandy, and drenched it with a rich butter sauce. The Italian version might be described as more heartfelt and rustic, the French way, more refined and complex. At Macrina we appreciate both schools of thought—but we favor the Italian ways by choosing locally available, high-quality, seasonal ingredients; using age-old cooking traditions; and finishing with simple presentations.

Before opening Macrina, I traveled through Italy on what I called a "bread pilgrimage," tasting the classics and regional specialties—and every bread product I could find. I sought out little bakeries tucked into alleyways, sometimes waiting in long lines for crackling, fragrant loaves just coming out of centuries-old ovens. (Think of the generations of families that frequented those bakeries!) My favorite bread was made at Panificio Arnese in Rome. The bread was barely shaped, the crust a deep bronze, the interior filled with irregular holes, and the sweet aroma intoxicating. It was baked in a hazelnut-fired brick oven. Many of the breads I tasted and fell in love with in Italy inspired the recipes we make at Macrina today.

This chapter begins with a recipe for Seed Dough, the master recipe and base for most of the recipes that follow. It's simply a mixture of flour, water, and yeast prepared several hours prior to making the bread dough. It's a short step, but oh, the flavor and texture benefits to your final baked loaf!

For a fun change of pace, you might like to try your hand at our Sardinian Flatbread, a crisp, thin cracker brushed with extra-virgin olive oil and sprinkled with truffle salt. Our Schiacciata, Piadina, Hightower Pane Francese, and Pugliese breads all have deep Italian roots. Their rustic, floury, and sometimes irregular appearances might fool you into thinking that their flavors are simple. Not so! The beautiful complex flavors of these loaves will surprise and delight your palate. Simply described, it's the Italian way.

Master Recipe: Seed Dough

1 cup filtered water, at room
temperature (about 65°F)

1 teaspoon active dry yeast

2 cups (9 ounces) unbleached
all-purpose flour

Seed dough gets its name from being the very first thing one makes when crafting a loaf of Italian-style bread. It's a short step that will add texture and complexity of flavor to your finished loaf. Essentially, it's a small amount of dough—a simple mix of water, yeast, and flour—that is prepared prior to making your bread dough. It rises for several hours, then rests in the refrigerator for a minimum of 12 hours. During that time, it starts the process called fermentation, developing a sponge-like texture and slightly sour aroma. Seed dough is used to make many of the loaves in this chapter—it's the base that gives most Italian-inspired breads their distinctive porous interior structure, and brings out the creamy, natural flavor of the wheat. It keeps refrigerated for 4 days but is at its best in the first 2 days (as it gets older the leavening power declines and the flavor becomes more sour). When ready to mix your bread ingredients, measure out the amount of seed dough called for in the recipe and let it warm at room temperature for about 30 minutes, then incorporate per recipe instructions.

MAKES 1¼ POUNDS (ENOUGH FOR 2 TO 4 LOAVES OF BREAD)

1. Pour the water into the bowl of a stand mixer fitted with the paddle attachment and sprinkle the yeast on top. Mix on low speed for 1 minute, or until the yeast has completely dissolved. Gradually add the flour and mix for about 2 minutes. (Or mix by hand, placing the water and yeast in a large bowl and whisking to dissolve the yeast, then adding the flour and mixing steadily for 3 minutes with a wooden spoon or rubber spatula.)

2. Lightly coat the inside of a large bowl with canola oil. Transfer the dough to the bowl and cover with plastic wrap. Let it rise in a warm place (approximately 75°F) for about 2 hours; the dough will double in size. (Don't be concerned if it hasn't quite doubled after 2 hours: the dough will hold its warmth and continue to rise a little after it's refrigerated.)

3. After the dough has risen, refrigerate it, still covered, for at least 12 hours to develop its flavors.

4. If you don't use all the seed dough from this recipe, you can freeze it for up to 2 weeks. Thaw, covered, for 2 to 3 hours, or until it reaches room temperature.

Pugliese

Pugliese bread originates from the Puglia region of Italy. Its dense texture and flavorful interior make it the quintessential Italian white bread. It's great for crostini or bruschetta and is stunning served simply as a table bread, with olive oil for dipping. If you'd like to try a heartier version of this bread, called pugliese integrale, *see the recipe variation that follows. It's made with coarse rye and whole wheat flours, which add a wonderful earthy, nutty quality to the bread as well as a deeply caramelized crust.*

MAKES ONE 10-INCH ROUND LOAF

1. Lightly oil a medium bowl with canola oil. Line a separate medium bowl with a clean cotton flour-sack towel and sprinkle it heavily with flour. Set aside. Fill a spray bottle with water and set aside.

2. In the bowl of a stand mixer fitted with the paddle attachment, mix the seed dough, water, and yeast on low speed for about 1 minute. (Or mix by hand, placing the ingredients in a large bowl and mixing with a wooden spoon to break up the seed dough.) Let the mixture sit for 3 minutes to activate the yeast.

3. Switch to the dough hook. Add the salt, then on low speed, gradually add the flour. When all the flour has been incorporated, increase the speed to medium and mix for 7 to 8 minutes. (If mixing by hand, add the salt and flour, and use a rubber spatula to mix until combined. Transfer the dough from the bowl onto a floured surface. Knead by hand for 8 minutes.) With floured fingers, pinch a big piece of dough and pull it away from the mass. It should stretch about 3 inches without tearing—it will feel a bit like a rubber band. If it doesn't pass this test, mix for another 1 to 3 minutes. Scrape the dough into the prepared bowl and cover with plastic wrap. Let it rise at warm room temperature (about 75°F) until doubled in size, about 2 hours.

4. Next, do a baker's turn on the dough (see Working with Wet Doughs, page 31). Re-cover the bowl with plastic wrap and let the dough rise again at room temperature until doubled in size, about another 2 hours.

5. After the dough has risen, gently pull it out onto a floured worked surface. Form the dough into a ball by folding each edge up toward the center. Flip the ball over and let it rest, seam side down, for several minutes to seal the base. Place the ball seam side up in the prepared towel-lined bowl. Cover it loosely with the edges of the towel and let

10 ounces (generous 1 cup) Seed Dough (page 22)

1½ cups filtered water, at room temperature (about 65°F)

½ teaspoon active dry yeast

2½ teaspoons kosher salt

3½ cups (1 pound) unbleached all-purpose flour

Cornmeal, for sprinkling the baker's peel

rise again for 1 hour at room temperature. The dough will be bouncy (almost like Jell-O) but will have enough strength to hold its shape once it is inverted onto the baker's peel.

6. About 20 minutes before baking, place a baking stone on the center rack of the oven and preheat to 450°F.

7. Sprinkle a baker's peel with cornmeal and invert the loaf onto it. With a sharp paring knife or razor blade, cut a 5-inch triangle design, about ⅛ inch deep, in the center of the loaf. Quickly slide the loaf onto the baking stone. Using the spray bottle, heavily mist the inside of the oven with water; the steam will help the loaf expand to its fullest potential before the crust sets. Mist twice more during the first 10 minutes of baking. Bake for 40 minutes, or until the bread is golden brown and sounds hollow when tapped on the bottom. Cool on a wire rack for at least 1 hour before serving.

�֍ ✣ ✣

VARIATION: PUGLIESE INTEGRALE

To make Pugliese Integrale, reduce the amount of all-purpose flour to 2 cups and add ¾ cup coarse rye flour and ¾ cup whole wheat flour. Also, because whole grain flours absorb more liquid than all-purpose flour, add an extra ⅓ cup water. Proceed with the recipe as written.

Piadina

Traveling in Italy, you're constantly tempted by espresso shops, cafés, and bars displaying loads and loads of premade sandwiches, each waiting to be placed on a hot panini grill. We offer a large assortment of sandwiches at our cafés as well, but we also wanted to offer a lighter sandwich alternative—and Piadina works beautifully in that role. A traditional thin, disklike flatbread from the Romagna region of Italy, it's typically folded in half and filled with any number of wonderful things—roasted vegetables, flavorful spreads, artisan cheeses, cured meats—and grilled before serving. Piadina is also great on appetizer plates: cut it into wedges and serve with spreads, olives, and assorted cheeses.

MAKES SEVEN 7-INCH ROUND FLATBREADS

5 ounces (generous ½ cup) Seed Dough (page 22)

¼ cup plus 1 tablespoon extra-virgin olive oil, divided

1 cup plus 1 tablespoon filtered water, at room temperature (about 65°F)

2¾ cups (12½ ounces) unbleached all-purpose flour

1½ teaspoons kosher salt

Cornmeal, for sprinkling the baker's peel

1. Lightly oil a medium bowl and a rimmed baking sheet with canola oil. Set aside.

2. In the bowl of a stand mixer fitted with the dough hook, mix the seed dough, ¼ cup of the olive oil, and water on low speed for 1 minute. Gradually add the flour and salt and mix until incorporated, then increase the speed to medium and mix for 6 to 8 minutes. The rather wet dough will pull away from the sides of the bowl but will still be tethered at the base. You will hear a slight slapping noise toward the end of the mixing time: this indicates the dough is the right consistency. Using a rubber spatula, scrape the dough into the prepared bowl and cover it with plastic wrap. Let the dough rise until it doubles in size, about 4 hours at room temperature.

3. Transfer the dough from the bowl onto a lightly floured work surface. Divide it into seven 4-ounce pieces. (If you don't have a scale, divide the dough as follows: Flatten the dough into a 7-by-4-inch rectangle. Cut a 1-by-4-inch strip off one end; then cut the remaining dough in half lengthwise. Divide each of these pieces into three 2-inch pieces.) A consistent size is important so the flatbreads bake evenly in the oven.

4. Form each piece into a ball by folding the edges up toward the center and flipping the piece over. Let it rest for several minutes, seam side down, to seal the base. Then cup the ball of dough in the palm of your hand, keeping your fingertips and the heel of your hand resting on the work surface. Move your hand in a circular motion. This will tighten the surface of the roll so it will rise evenly. (You'll notice that it's important to have just a light dusting of flour on your work surface—too

much and the dough will slide around; too little and it will refuse to do much besides stick to the tabletop.) Place the dough balls 3 inches apart on the prepared baking sheet. Brush the tops with the remaining 1 tablespoon olive oil and cover with plastic wrap. Let the dough rise for 2 hours at room temperature.

5. About 20 minutes before baking, place a baking stone on the center rack of the oven and preheat to 450°F.

6. Place one of the dough balls on a floured work surface. Flatten it with your hands, and then, using a rolling pin, roll it out into a 7-inch disk. Set aside and roll the remaining disks. Sprinkle a baker's peel with cornmeal and place one disk on it. Slide it onto the baking stone; depending on the size of your stone, you may be able to place one more beside it. Bake for 4 minutes on one side, then flip; using the baker's peel, press down on the bread to remove any air bubbles. Bake for another 3 minutes. This bread will be very pliable, and even though it's baked all the way through, it will not brown very much. Repeat with the remaining disks.

7. Store any leftovers in plastic wrap to retain their softness. They will keep for 3 days at room temperature. Wrapped well, they'll freeze nicely for up to 3 weeks.

Schiacciata

This is a Tuscan flatbread made with a generous amount of olive oil, similar to focaccia. Because of the olive oil, and because it's stretched when placed on the hot baking stone, it transforms into a thin, flaky flatbread. This is a favorite topped with tapenade, roasted artichoke spread, or hummus finished with crumbled goat cheese and fresh herbs. Schiacciata is also often split and made into a rich, delicious sandwich-type snack—either way, it's the perfect accompaniment to an aperitivo *shared with your friends.*

MAKES THREE 8-BY-4-INCH FLATBREADS

6 ounces (¾ cup) Seed Dough (page 22)

1½ cups filtered water

1 teaspoon active dry yeast

½ cup plus 3 tablespoons extra-virgin olive oil, divided

1 tablespoon chopped assorted fresh herbs (parsley, oregano, basil, chives, rosemary)

2¼ teaspoons kosher salt

3½ cups (1 pound) unbleached all-purpose flour

Cornmeal, for sprinkling the baker's peel

1½ teaspoons coarse sea salt, for garnish

1. Lightly oil a medium bowl with canola oil. Line a rimmed baking sheet with a clean cotton flour-sack towel and sprinkle it heavily with flour. Set aside. Fill a spray bottle with water and set aside.

2. In the bowl of a stand mixer fitted with the paddle attachment, mix the seed dough, water, and yeast on low speed for about 1 minute. Switch to the dough hook and add ½ cup of the olive oil, herbs, and kosher salt. Gradually add the flour and mix until incorporated, then increase the speed to medium and mix for 6 to 8 minutes. Toward the end of the mixing time, you'll hear the dough slapping against the side of the bowl; this indicates the dough is the right consistency. With floured fingers, pinch a big piece of dough and pull it away from the mass. It should stretch about 3 inches without tearing—it will feel a bit like a rubber band. If it tears, mix for another 1 to 3 minutes.

3. Turn out the dough onto a floured work surface and form it into a ball. Transfer the dough to the prepared bowl and cover with plastic wrap. Let the dough rise for about 1½ hours, or until it has doubled in size.

4. Next, do a baker's turn on the dough (see Working with Wet Doughs, page 31). Re-cover with plastic wrap and let the dough rise again at room temperature for another hour.

5. After the dough has risen, invert the bowl onto a well-floured work surface, letting the dough drop gently. Working carefully in order to deflate the dough as little as possible, form it into an 8-by-12-inch rectangle. This dough is wet, so use plenty of flour to make sure it doesn't stick. Cut the dough crosswise into 3 equal pieces (they will each form a rectangle approximately 8 by 4 inches). Lift the dough pieces onto the prepared towel, pulling it up to form two 1-inch "walls" that separate

the loaves. (There's no need to cover them—you actually want them to dry out a little so they're easier to transfer to the oven.) Let rise again for 45 minutes; the dough will be spongy to the touch. About halfway through this final rise, place a baking stone on the center rack of the oven and preheat to 425°F.

6. Lift each loaf gently and flip it over, placing it back on the towel. Sprinkle the baker's peel with the cornmeal, then transfer the loaves, slightly stretching each one as you lift it onto the baker's peel. Keep the thickness of the dough as even as possible while retaining its rectangular shape. Dimple the dough with your fingertips. Quickly slide the loaves onto the preheated baking stone, spacing them 1 inch apart. (Depending on the size of your baking stone, you should be able to bake all 3 loaves at once. If there is room for only 2 loaves, cover the extra loaf and let it rest at room temperature until the others are finished baking.) Using the spray bottle, heavily mist the inside of the oven with water; the steam will help the loaves expand to their fullest potential before the crusts set. Mist twice more during the first 10 minutes of baking. Bake for 20 to 25 minutes, or until the loaves are golden brown. Cool on a wire rack; after 10 minutes, brush the tops with the remaining 3 tablespoons olive oil (about 1 tablespoon each) and sprinkle them with the sea salt.

7. Schiacciata are best the day they are baked. If you have leftovers, wrap them in plastic and store them at room temperature for another day. Cut them horizontally, fill them with your choice of cheeses, meats, olives, or vegetables, and grill them for an awesome sandwich.

❖ Working *with* Wet Doughs ❖

For bread that begins with a very wet dough, you don't want to develop the gluten too much. If you were to knead the dough (whether by hand or in a stand mixer) to the point of full gluten development, it would become too warm, and the flavor of the wheat would be blanched out. Once baked, the interior crumb would be overly white, and the crust would take on a gray, cloudy color with an overly thick texture. Instead, you want to knead it lightly in the beginning and later, to complete the gluten development, do what we call a "baker's turn." The resulting loaf will bake to a deep golden-brown color with complex flavors and a beautiful, cream-colored interior.

Here's how to do a baker's turn:

1. Flour your hands well. Keeping the dough in the bowl, use your fingertips to release the edges of the dough from the bowl.

2. Stretch the dough outward: first pull the right side, extending the dough out past the rim of the bowl approximately 6 inches. Bring the stretched dough back to the center of the bowl and lay it back on top.

3. Do the same with the left side and the top and bottom portions of the dough, bringing the stretched dough back to the center each time. (See photo, opposite.)

4. Flip the dough ball over, placing it seam side down in the bowl.

5. Now you're ready to proceed according to recipe instructions.

Hightower Pane Francese

FOR THE BIGA STARTER:

1 cup filtered water, at room temperature (about 65°F)

1 teaspoon active dry yeast

½ cup (2¼ ounces) unbleached all-purpose flour

½ cup (2¼ ounces) stone-ground whole wheat flour

FOR THE DOUGH:

Biga starter

1½ cups lukewarm filtered water (about 80°F)

¼ teaspoon active dry yeast

2 teaspoons amber agave syrup

4 cups (18 ounces) unbleached all-purpose flour

2¼ teaspoons kosher salt

Cornmeal, for sprinkling the baker's peel

I first had a version of this bread at the San Francisco Baking Institute, and I loved its airy, slightly sour interior; lovely thin, floured-streaked caramel-brown crust; and baguette-like size—perfect for making small sandwiches or crostini. At Macrina, we make this loaf with a natural starter that uses Hightower Cellars' cabernet sauvignon grapes. For this version, you'll make a biga starter—which is, in fact, the more traditional method. Take a few minutes to make the biga the evening before you wish to make the bread—it adds so much complexity of flavor to the finished loaf.

MAKES TWO 4-BY-12-INCH LOAVES

1. Make the biga starter the night before you wish to make the bread. Pour the water into a medium bowl, sprinkle the yeast on top, and whisk to dissolve the yeast. Gradually add the flours and whisk for about 3 minutes to break up any lumps and begin developing the gluten. Cover the bowl with plastic wrap and let it sit at room temperature for a minimum of 10 hours. If you wish to hold the biga starter longer than 24 hours, refrigerate it to slow down the fermentation. The biga will keep for up to 4 days in the refrigerator, but it will develop a more sour taste as the fermentation continues—this adds to the biga's acidity, which in turn lessens its leavening power. Therefore, for best results, I prefer to use the biga within 2 days of making it.

2. Lightly oil a medium bowl with canola oil. Line a rimmed baking sheet with a clean cotton flour-sack towel and sprinkle it heavily with flour. Set aside. Fill a spray bottle with water and set aside.

3. To make the dough, using a rubber spatula, scoop the biga into the bowl of a stand mixer fitted with the dough hook. Add the water, yeast, and agave syrup, and mix on low speed for 1 minute. Gradually add the flour and salt; when all the flour has been incorporated, increase the speed to medium and mix for 12 minutes. Toward the end of the mixing time, you'll hear the dough slapping against the side of the bowl; this is an indication that the dough is the right consistency. With floured fingers, pinch a big piece of dough and pull it away from the mass. It should stretch about 3 inches without tearing—it will feel a bit like a rubber band. If it tears, mix for another 1 to 3 minutes. Using a rubber spatula, transfer the dough into the prepared bowl and cover with plastic wrap. Let it rise at room temperature until it has almost doubled in size, about 2 hours.

4. Next, do a baker's turn on the dough (see Working with Wet Doughs, page 31). Re-cover with plastic wrap and let the dough rise again at room temperature for another 2 hours.

5. After the dough has risen, invert the bowl onto a well-floured work surface and gently pull out the dough. Shape it into an 8-by-12-inch rectangle, then halve it lengthwise, creating 2 baguette-shaped loaves. (One of this loaf's characteristics is the irregular hole structure in its interior, so don't overmanipulate the dough. Your goal is to have a fairly consistent thickness so it will bake evenly—but keep those random air pockets.) Place the loaves on the prepared towel, spacing them 2 inches apart. Pull the towel up in the middle to form a "wall" between the loaves (see photo, page 11). (There's no need to cover them—you actually want them to dry out a little so they're easier to transfer to the oven.) Let the loaves rise for another 30 minutes.

6. About 20 minutes before baking, place a baking stone on the center rack of the oven and preheat to 450°F.

7. Sprinkle a baker's peel with cornmeal. Using both hands, pick up the first loaf and flip it over so that the floured side is facing up. Repeat with the second loaf. Quickly place the loaves on the baker's peel and load onto the baking stone, spacing them 2 inches apart. Using the spray bottle, heavily mist the inside of the oven with water; the steam will help the loaves expand to their fullest potential before the crusts set. Mist twice more during the first 10 minutes of baking. Bake for 30 minutes, or until the loaves are deep golden brown and sound hollow when tapped on the bottom. Cool on a wire rack for 20 minutes before serving. The loaves can be stored at room temperature for up to 3 days wrapped in plastic.

Sardinian Flatbread with Truffle Salt

1½ cups (7½ ounces) semolina flour, plus extra for sprinkling

1½ cups (6¾ ounces) unbleached all-purpose flour

1 tablespoon chopped fresh rosemary

1½ teaspoons kosher salt

¾ cup filtered water

½ cup extra-virgin olive oil, divided

1½ teaspoons truffle salt (found in specialty stores)

We've been making Sardinian Flatbread since our opening in 1993. This flavorful, crisp cracker comes from a hand-mixed dough that uses semolina flour, fresh rosemary, and olive oil. It's made much like pasta dough and can be either rolled out thinly by hand or cranked through a pasta machine—thus its Italian name, carta da musica, *or "sheet music," referring to its thinness. A supplier brought the truffle salt by the bakery one day, and I thought it would be the perfect addition to this flatbread.*

MAKES 20 LARGE CRACKERS

1. Flour a rimmed baking sheet and set aside.

2. Whisk the flours, rosemary, and kosher salt in a large bowl to evenly distribute. Make a well in the center of the bowl and pour in the water and ¼ cup of the olive oil. With a rubber spatula, begin drawing the dry ingredients into the liquids. Continue bringing in the dry ingredients until a dough starts to form. (This process, very similar to how pasta dough is traditionally made, could also be done on your work surface—but I find it works best to contain the dough in the bowl.)

3. Using your hands, knead the dough for 5 minutes by folding it onto itself, making a ball, then folding it in on itself again. The dough will become smoother, and you'll get a little "push back" when you press your finger into it. Form the ball into a 4-by-10-inch rectangle and place it on the prepared baking sheet. Cover the sheet with plastic wrap and refrigerate for at least 2 hours.

4. About 20 minutes before baking, place a baking stone on the center rack of the oven and preheat to 425°F.

5. With a knife, divide the dough into 10 equal pieces.

6. Choose to make the crackers by hand or with a pasta machine.

To make the crackers by hand, cut all of the dough pieces in half. Flatten each piece into a rectangular shape and, using a rolling pin and extra flour as needed, roll until the dough is paper-thin. The shape of the hand-rolled pieces will not be rectangular and uniform, as with a pasta machine, but slightly oval and irregular. Make sure each piece is not too big to fit on your baking stone.

To make the crackers with a pasta machine, flatten each piece into a rectangular shape with a rolling pin. Set the rollers on the widest setting (usually #1) and slowly feed the first piece of dough through the rollers. (Keep the other pieces covered to keep them from drying out.) Fold the ends of the dough into the center and pass it through the rollers again, still on the widest setting. (This will help keep it in the correct shape for making multiple passes through the pasta machine.) Dust the dough with flour if necessary to prevent sticking.

Turn the dial to the next (narrower) setting and continue feeding the dough through the machine. Repeat this procedure with each setting, stopping at #4. Cut the dough crosswise in half—these smaller pieces will be easier to work with.

Continue passing the dough through the pasta machine. Take your time and feed the dough in straight to prevent folding and tearing. I also create a little tension on the dough by pulling back as it goes through the rollers; this helps prevent creases. The final size of each flatbread at setting #8 will be about 15 by 5 inches. As you finish rolling each piece of dough, layer the pieces on a baking sheet, separating them with a piece of parchment paper and a dusting of semolina flour until you are ready to start baking.

7. Transfer a piece of the flattened dough to the baking stone by hand or slide it in using a baker's peel. (Depending on how comfortable you feel maneuvering the flatbread, you can fill up the stone—just make sure the crackers are in a single layer, with no folds or overlap.) Bake for 1 to 2 minutes, or until the flatbread is golden brown and slightly bubbled. Cool on a wire rack for 5 minutes. Gently brush the flatbreads with the remaining ¼ cup olive oil and sprinkle lightly with the truffle salt. The flatbreads will stay crisp for up to a week stored in a dry container.

❋ Bread *and* Wine: A Serendipitous Story ❋

A few years ago I made my way eastward from Seattle, three-and-a-half hours across the state, to the dry desert country where Washington's premier vineyards and wineries preside. Near the winding Yakima River, with Horse Heaven Hills in the distance, I discovered Hightower Cellars winery. Hightower Cellars is in the esteemed Red Mountain appellation (Washington's smallest, named after its unusual red-hued grass). True, the winery's adorable mascot, a yellow Lab pictured on the label of several of their bottlings, drew me in—but it was the generosity of the winemakers, Tim and Kelly Hightower, that really captured my attention. They are both amazingly gifted winemakers, and their fun, understated presence makes asking questions a breeze. And oh, the wine is so delicious!

In 2010 Tim and Kelly called me with a "wild hair of an idea." They were interested in offering me some cabernet sauvignon wine grapes that I could use to make a sour bread starter (sourdough starters can be developed from the natural yeasts found on grape skins, adding leavening and superb flavor). I decided to create a bread from this starter that the Hightowers could use for tasting and entertaining at their winery, and that we could offer in our cafés. After a number of baking trials and tweaks, our Pane Francese was born: an Italian version of a crusty baguette: batonlike, with a light, porous crumb and a crisp, caramel-brown crust. We "broke bread" together, declared it a smashing success, and have since paired their wines with our bread at numerous events and occasions. I love it when fate intervenes and people come together to create something brand new.

I wanted to share my great experiences at Hightower Cellars with some of our key Macrina staff, so recently about fifteen of us organized a little sojourn to the winery. Arriving just as the sun was setting over the hills, we were greeted warmly and immediately swept into Hightower's intimate tasting room to sample six of Tim and Kelly's wines. There was their Murray Syrah (named after that handsome yellow Lab); Out of Line Red Wine, made with grapes planted at a unique slanted angle for best sun exposure; and their prestigious merlot and cabernet sauvignon bottlings. We also had the pleasure of tasting several grape varietals straight from the barrel. I thought blending wine was for overall flavor enhancement, but they were very good standing alone!

This kicked off a fantastic day and a half of delicious food, interesting stories, vineyard walks, and new friendships. This wasn't a marketing package designed to promote either of our businesses, but a genuine, heartfelt opportunity to learn how other artisan industries operate, and to enjoy one other's company.

Who would have imagined that the making of a simple bread starter would lead to such inspiring new experiences? It's something our staff still talks about: the serendipitous way creative, passionate, hardworking people can bring out the best in each other.

ARTISANAL
BREADS

SINCE WRITING MY FIRST COOKBOOK, my greatest reward has been hearing readers tell their stories of happy successes with so many recipes. This chapter is based on three recipes that I make at home all the time, and I feel sure they'll become favorites for many of you. First, you'll learn how to make very flavorful artisan bread by using a technique that's somewhat new in the bread-baking world: the no-knead method. You won't have to rely on a homemade starter to build flavor, plus you have the ease of mixing and letting the dough rise in the same bowl. Formed simply into a ball, the dough rises for the last time and is then baked in a heavy dutch oven.

Why bake bread in a big cast-iron pot with a lid? Because one of the keys to baking a beautiful artisan loaf is having a humid atmosphere when the bread first hits the oven. The moist air inside the covered pot keeps the bread's outer surface soft for the first few minutes of baking, allowing it to rise before it forms a hard crust. The result is a really beautiful loaf—domed, crusty, caramelized to a deep brown color, and full of complex flavors. I've found that baking in a cast-iron pot creates the all-time best results for home bread baking.

Try both versions of our dutch oven artisan bread: the One-Day Artisan Loaf and One-Day Artisan Whole Grain Loaf. The technique is the same, but the flavors and ingredients are different: the former uses olive oil and milk in the dough to add a slight fermented flavor, and the latter is a heartier, earthier whole grain version made with rye and whole wheat flours. The pizza crust recipe uses a similar base formula. I like to cook it on a hot barbecue because the grill marks on the crust and subtle smoky flavor are reminiscent of pizzas baked in Italian wood-burning ovens.

For those of you who've always wanted to bake homemade bread but feel something holding you back, these recipes can be your place to start. Making a wonderful crusty loaf or a homemade pizza crust is definitely within your grasp: start this dough in the morning at 10, and you'll be breaking bread with friends and family by dinner!

One-Day Artisan Loaf

This bread was inspired by a November 2006 article in the New York Times *featuring Sullivan Street Bakery owner Jim Lahey. He developed a rather revolutionary method of creating a beautiful, crusty, full-flavored, artisan-style bread that is made in a relatively short time, mixed entirely by hand, and completed without a bit of kneading. I've developed my own version, adding just the right combination of ingredients to make it even more flavorful. I make this bread often to take to dinner parties when it's not convenient to stop by Macrina.*

MAKES ONE 9-INCH ROUND LOAF

¾ cup milk

¾ cup filtered water

2 teaspoons active dry yeast

¼ cup extra-virgin olive oil

2½ cups (11¼ ounces) unbleached all-purpose flour

½ cup (2 ounces) stone-ground rye flour

2 teaspoons kosher salt

1. Line a medium bowl with a clean cotton flour-sack towel and sprinkle it heavily with flour. Set aside.

2. Combine the milk and water in a medium saucepan. Warm to about 80°F (barely warm to the touch) and pour into a medium bowl. Sprinkle the yeast over the surface of the liquid and whisk gently until it has dissolved. Let the mixture sit for about 3 minutes to activate the yeast.

3. Add the olive oil, flours, and salt. Using a rubber spatula, mix the ingredients by pulling the spatula through the dough and flipping it over to simulate a kneading motion. Continue mixing and folding for 2 to 3 minutes. The dough will have no more flour pockets and will be quite wet. Cover with plastic wrap and let the dough rise for 2 hours at warm room temperature (75 to 80°F), or until the dough has doubled in size.

4. Lightly sprinkle the top of the dough with flour (this dough is very sticky). Next, do a baker's turn on the dough (see Working with Wet Doughs, page 31). Re-cover the bowl with plastic wrap and let the dough rise again at room temperature for 1 hour.

5. Once the dough has risen, refrigerate it, still covered in the bowl, for 2 to 3 hours (this slows the rate at which the dough rises; the longer fermentation period will result in more flavorful bread).

6. Transfer the dough from the bowl onto a floured work surface and do another baker's turn—this time on your work surface rather than in the bowl. Invert the loaf so that it's seam side down. Cup your hands around the dough ball, resting the outer portion of your hands on the

work surface. Move the ball in a circular motion to tighten it at the base. Invert the rounded loaf again and place it seam side up in the towel-lined bowl; lightly cover the top with the overhanging towel. Let it rise at room temperature until it is about 1½ times its original size, 2 to 3 hours.

7. One hour before baking, preheat the oven to 450°F. Choose to make the bread in a double or standard dutch oven. Place the cast-iron dutch oven, with its lid, inside to preheat.

To bake the bread in a double dutch oven (no handle on the lid), carefully remove the preheated lid and place it upside down on the stovetop. Tip the bowl so that the proofed loaf falls gently out into the lid. Slowly remove the cloth (the dough may stick here and there). With a sharp paring knife or razor blade, cut a ⅛-inch-deep, 4-inch square shape on the top of the loaf. Being sure to use oven mitts, quickly retrieve the deep part of the dutch oven and cover the unbaked loaf. (You are basically using the double dutch oven upside down.) Put the whole pot, with the bread inside, into the oven.

To bake the bread in a standard dutch oven (with a handle on the lid), first flip the loaf onto your work surface. Slowly remove the cloth (the dough may stick here and there). With a sharp paring knife or razor blade, cut a ⅛-inch-deep, 4-inch square shape on the top of the loaf. Being sure to use oven mitts, quickly retrieve the dutch oven and remove the lid. Gently place the loaf into the deep part of the dutch oven, being careful not to burn your fingers or forearms on the sides of the hot pan. Cover the pan with the lid and place in the oven.

* Dutch Ovens *

Dutch ovens are those heavy, deep, cast-iron roasting pots with equally heavy, tight-fitting lids that are used for slow, moist cooking—you may have used one to braise a scrumptious pork shoulder or simmer a pot of chili or stew. They come in two basic styles; probably the most common has a lid with a handle on top. But there's another style that works fabulously for the breads in this chapter: its lid looks like an upside-down sauté pan. They both work well for bread baking, but I recommend the latter style because it's much easier to load the loaf into and handle in a hot oven. It's called a double dutch oven: you can order it online (see Resources, page 219) or perhaps find one at your favorite antiques store.

8.   Bake for 30 minutes, then remove the top. Continue baking until the loaf is deep brown and very crusty, about another 20 minutes.

9.   If baking in a double dutch oven, transfer the loaf with your hands (using oven mitts) to a wire rack to cool. (If using a standard dutch oven, simply flip the loaf out onto the wire rack.) In both cases the bread should release easily from the pan. As it cools, the crust will soften a bit, and the interior will be very moist. Let the loaf cool completely (about 1 hour) before cutting.

One-Day Artisan Whole Grain Loaf

1¾ cups lukewarm filtered water (about 80°F)

2 tablespoons amber agave syrup

2 teaspoons active dry yeast

1¼ cups (5½ ounces) unbleached all-purpose flour

1 cup (4½ ounces) stone-ground whole wheat flour

½ cup (2 ounces) stone-ground rye flour

2 teaspoons kosher salt

I really love the extra dimension of flavor that whole grains bring to bread. They have a nuttiness and an earthiness you just don't get from all-purpose flour. In this loaf, I even detect notes of apple cider and hints of pineapple. This deep brown, crusty loaf works well at any dinner table—but it's particularly good with a hearty winter soup. With the addition of agave syrup to this dough, it will be one of the prettiest loaves you've ever baked!

MAKES ONE 9-INCH ROUND LOAF

1. Line a medium bowl with a clean cotton flour-sack towel and sprinkle it heavily with flour. Set aside.

2. Combine the water and agave syrup in a large bowl. Sprinkle the yeast over the surface of the liquid and whisk gently until it has dissolved. Let the mixture sit for about 3 minutes to activate the yeast.

3. Add the flours and salt. Using a rubber spatula, mix the ingredients for 2 to 3 minutes by pulling the spatula through the dough and flipping it over to simulate a kneading motion. The dough will have no more flour pockets and will be quite wet. Cover the bowl with plastic wrap and let the dough rise for 2 hours at warm room temperature (75 to 80°F), or until the dough has doubled in size.

4. Lightly sprinkle the top of the dough with flour (this dough is very sticky). Do a baker's turn on the dough (see Working with Wet Doughs, page 31). Re-cover the bowl with plastic wrap and let the dough rise again at room temperature for another 2 hours.

5. When the dough has risen, do a second baker's turn. Again, re-cover the bowl with plastic wrap and let the dough rise at room temperature for another hour.

6. Transfer the dough onto a floured work surface and do a third baker's turn—this time on your work surface rather than in the bowl. Invert the loaf so that it is seam side down, then cup your hands around the dough ball, resting the outer portion of your hands on the work surface. Move the ball in a circular motion to tighten it at the base. Invert the rounded loaf again and place it seam side up in the towel-lined bowl; lightly cover the top with the overhanging towel. Let it rise at room temperature until it is about 1½ times its original size, about 1 hour. (This loaf should have a texture like Jell-O, that is, slightly

underproofed. If it has risen too much at this stage, it will collapse when you place it in the dutch oven.)

7. One hour before baking, preheat the oven to 450°F. Choose to make the bread in a double or standard dutch oven. Place the cast-iron dutch oven, with its lid, inside to preheat.

To bake the bread in a double dutch oven (no handle on the lid), carefully remove the preheated lid and place it upside down on the stovetop. Tip the bowl so that the proofed loaf falls gently out into the lid. Slowly remove the cloth (the dough may stick here and there). With a sharp paring knife or razor blade, cut a ⅛-inch-deep, 4-inch square on the top of the loaf. Being sure to use oven mitts, quickly retrieve the deep part of the dutch oven and cover the unbaked loaf. (You are basically using the double dutch oven upside down.) Put the whole pot, with the bread inside, into the oven.

To bake the bread in a standard dutch oven (with a handle on the lid), flip the loaf onto your floured work surface. Slowly remove the cloth (the dough may stick here and there). With a sharp paring knife or razor blade, cut a ⅛-inch-deep, 4-inch square on the top of the loaf. Being sure to use oven mitts, quickly retrieve the dutch oven and remove the lid. Gently drop the loaf into the deep part of the dutch oven, being careful not to burn your fingers or forearms on the sides of the hot pan. Cover the pan with the lid and place in the oven.

8. Bake for 30 minutes, then remove the top. Continue baking until the loaf is deep brown and very crusty, about another 20 minutes.

9. If baking in a double dutch oven, transfer the loaf with your hands (using oven mitts) to a wire rack to cool. (If using a standard dutch oven, simply flip the loaf out onto the wire rack.) In both cases the bread should release easily from the pan. Let the loaf cool completely (about 1 hour) before cutting.

✣ Whole Grain Milling:
A Revolution *in the* Right Direction ✣

Last year I visited Craig Ponsford, a remarkable baker from Sonoma, California, and past chairman of the Bread Bakers Guild of America. He shared a story about his experiences baking with whole grain milled flour, a product that's fueling a small revolution in the world of artisan bread baking.

What most people—even serious bakers—don't realize when they buy "whole grain" or "whole wheat" flour is that it's not truly whole at all. Most often, it's flour that's made using a process that breaks the grain into its main components (endosperm, bran, and germ), strips away the most nutritious parts, and then either further refines the carbohydrate-rich part as white flour or adds a bit of the bran and germ back (typically 15 to 35 percent) to make the product "whole."

True whole grain milling—where the flour, with its many complex flavors and nutrients, is made from grain that's milled intact and *left* intact—is creating excitement among dedicated artisan bakers such as Craig. His several years of experimentation and research have shown that this true whole grain flour is stable (it doesn't spoil easily, as was previously believed would happen if the wheat germ was left in the flour mix) and—most important—it makes astonishingly good baked goods, from beautiful breads to pizza crusts to pastries.

Craig's stories and enthusiasm intrigued me. I started asking questions of the mills whose flours we use. To my pleasant surprise, one of the local mills we've supported over the years—Fairhaven Organic Flour Mill, located about an hour north of Seattle—practices whole grain milling. Started as a cooperative in 1974, Fairhaven is now owned by Kevin and Matsuko Christenson, who took it over in 2007. Since then, they've been building the business step by step. I could sense Kevin's sincere commitment when he told me the efforts they make to stick to their credo: buy only locally grown, organic grains; maintain loyalty to each farmer; and mill the grains only in small quantities so they are as nutrient-rich as possible.

On a recent tour, Kevin showed me his two mills (three, actually, counting the stone grinder that dates from 1945). The machines make flour by first cracking the grain through a blur of hammer blades. Then the miller chooses among a collection of screens, from coarse to very fine, to get the perfect consistency for that particular flour. Kevin describes his freshly milled flour as "alive." Passing your hand through a bag of it, you believe him. The texture is beautiful, and there's a weight to this flour—a slight moistness—not found in airy, overly dried commercial flours. You can smell the natural sweetness and complex characteristics of the whole grains. For me, the proof is in the product: the artisan breads we produce with Fairhaven's flours—Vollkorn Bread (page 5), Hightower Pane Francese (page 32), and Greek Olive Bread, to name just a few—have exceptional flavor and texture.

The Christensons' passion for their business centers on making a positive impact in the community by creating connections that support other local businesses and economies. Kevin says he's become increasingly aware of the health connection his flour provides. "It's not a boutique food product—it's food for the people."

Grilled Pizza Crusts

This is my personal go-to recipe for pizza crusts. It mixes much like the One-Day Artisan Bread but with a few different ingredients, so it creates a unique finished product. The little bit of sugar in the dough encourages the crust to bake to a deep golden brown. I'm a huge fan of cooking these pizza crusts on your barbecue or a ridged, cast-iron grill pan, but you can also use a baking stone for a more traditional result.

MAKES FOUR 8-INCH PIZZA CRUSTS

¾ cup lukewarm whole milk (about 80°F)

¾ cup lukewarm filtered water (about 80°F)

1½ teaspoons sugar

2 teaspoons active dry yeast

2 tablespoons extra-virgin olive oil

2½ cups plus 2 tablespoons (11½ ounces) unbleached all-purpose flour

2 tablespoons stone-ground whole wheat flour

2 teaspoons kosher salt

1. Line a rimmed baking sheet with parchment paper and brush it lightly with a mild-flavored olive oil. Set aside.

2. Combine the milk and water in a medium mixing bowl. Add the sugar, then sprinkle the yeast over the surface of the liquid. Using a whisk, dissolve the sugar and yeast. Let the mixture sit for about 3 minutes to activate the yeast.

3. Add the olive oil, flours, and salt. With a rubber spatula , mix the ingredients for 2 to 3 minutes by pulling the spatula through the dough and flipping it over to simulate a kneading motion. The dough will be free of lumps but will be shaggy and look wet—not like typical kneaded dough. Cover the bowl with plastic wrap and let the dough rise until it has doubled in size, 2 to 2½ hours at room temperature.

4. Lightly sprinkle the top of the dough with flour. Do a baker's turn on the dough (see Working with Wet Doughs, page 31). Re-cover the bowl with plastic wrap and let the dough rise again at warm room temperature (75 to 80°F) for another 30 minutes.

5. Once the dough has risen, refrigerate it, still covered in the bowl, for 2 hours (this slows the rate at which the dough rises; the longer fermentation period will result in more flavorful pizza crust).

6. Sprinkle the dough lightly with flour. Invert the bowl onto a well-floured work surface and gently pull out the dough. Using a bench knife or a plastic scraper, divide the dough into 4 equal pieces. Form each piece into a rough ball by folding the edges into the center. Flip the balls over so that the seam sides are down. Cup your hand over a dough

ball, resting your fingertips on the work surface. Move the ball in a circular motion to tighten it at the base. Set it aside and continue with the remaining balls. Arrange the dough balls 3 inches apart on the prepared baking sheet, brush the tops lightly with oil, and cover the baking sheet with plastic wrap. (The dough may be made to this point and stored in the refrigerator overnight, where it will rise slowly. This will make the dough more flavorful—as well as easier to handle. Flatten the balls the next day as instructed.)

7. Let the dough rise at room temperature until doubled in size and soft to the touch, about 2 hours.

8. Using your hands or a rolling pin, flatten each ball, starting from the center. Pick up the flattened dough and, again working your way out from the center, pinch and flatten some more, rotating the disk as you go. Your goal is to stretch the dough into an 8-inch circle. I like to leave the edges a little thicker to hold in the delicious toppings.

9. Choose one of the following ways to cook your pizza.

To grill the pizza on a gas barbecue, preheat the barbecue to 450°F (or high on the dial). The grate must be clean and very hot before grilling the pizzas—to minimize sticking, brush it with vegetable oil both before heating and before you cook the pizza dough. Lift the pizza crusts onto the barbecue. Cook them for about 2 minutes on each side, flipping them with tongs. Brush more oil on the grate if the dough is sticking.

Top with a few favorite ingredients. Lower the temperature to 350°F (or medium on the dial), close the top, and bake for another 6 to 8 minutes. During this time, your toppings will heat, any cheeses will melt, and the crust will be grilled crispy but not charred black. If you notice the pizza cooking too quickly, lower the temperature, lift the pizzas to a hanging shelf above the grill, or move them to an oven to finish cooking.

To bake the pizza on a cast-iron grill pan, preheat the oven to 450°F and set the pan inside. Line 2 baking sheets with parchment paper and set aside. When the oven has heated, carefully set one of the crusts on top of the grill pan. Bake for 2 minutes, then flip it over with tongs and bake for another 2 to 3 minutes. Transfer the crust from the oven to the baking sheet and top with a few favorite ingredients; repeat with the other 3 crusts.

Reduce the oven temperature to 400°F and bake for 5 to 8 minutes, or until the toppings are very hot and any cheeses are beginning to bubble and brown.

❧ Pizza Toppings ❧

Here are a few of my favorite topping combinations, listed in the order you'd put them on the crust. Remember, the integrity of your ingredients is everything. And simple is often best.

1. Brush the crust with olive oil, then spread it with whole milk goat ricotta cheese from Amaltheia Organic Dairy (found in specialty stores such as Whole Foods). Add sliced artisan salami, sliced heirloom tomatoes, and chèvre. After the pizza comes off the grill or out of the oven, top it with a generous handful of fresh arugula, then drizzle with olive oil, a splash of balsamic vinegar, and a sprinkle of salt.

2. Coat the crust with cooled alfredo sauce, then top with roasted leeks, grated Pecorino Romano cheese, and thinly sliced prosciutto. After the pizza comes off the grill or out of the oven, top it with a drizzle of extra-virgin olive oil, a chiffonade (ribbons) of fresh basil, and a scatter of coarse sea salt.

3. Spread the crust with a simple red sauce, then add grilled sweet onions, grilled asparagus, chopped green olives, and crumbled *fromage blanc* (my favorite is from Mt. Townsend Creamery). Finish it with a sprinkle of nice sea salt, some cracked pepper, and a drizzle of extra-virgin olive oil.

SWEET BREADS

IT'S SAID THAT BRIOCHE EVOLVED centuries ago, likely in France, from the "blessed bread" offered in churches. While its origins may be quite simple, over the last several hundred years bakers and pastry chefs have transformed brioche by adding what are now standard ingredients: eggs, butter, and sugar. Thus, modern brioche has the intriguing distinction of retaining both bread and cake characteristics. Once you've baked it at home, you'll understand its intoxicating powers: the sweet smells of vanilla, eggs, yeast, butter, and sugar melding together in the oven; the warm golden color of the finished bread; and the rich, complex flavors that will stop you in your tracks. Brioche—also commonly known as French breakfast bread—is used for many of our most popular pastries, sweet and savory alike.

This chapter starts with the master recipe for Sweet Brioche Dough, which is the base for all the recipes that follow. Note that in all cases, this dough needs about three hours to rise, so plan your time accordingly. Brioche dough can be made the night before, refrigerated, and then pulled out about two hours before it's needed the next day. In addition to being convenient, the overnight rest helps the dough build deeper flavors by providing an environment where its organic acids can develop without the dough rising too much.

Here's a sneak peek at a few of the recipes in this collection using Sweet Brioche Dough. Sugar Buns are just flat-out impossible to resist: they're a cross between a cheese Danish and a raised sugar doughnut. Cocoa Puffs come with a fun surprise: the dough is baked in muffin pans with a generous dollop of chocolate ganache hidden in the middle. Also included is the recipe for a year-round favorite at the bakery: the Apple Cinnamon Pull-Apart—sophisticated enough for discerning foodies, but with familiar flavors that kids love, too.

I'm amazed at the versatility of this brioche dough. I've offered just a few ideas for ways to use it, but you can probably think of many more. And you don't have to limit your creations to sweet items—this dough also works beautifully with savory ingredients such as ham and gruyère cheese, or sautéed spinach and roasted red peppers. This is what baking's all about—the many possibilities.

Master Recipe: Sweet Brioche Dough

¼ cup lukewarm filtered water (about 80°F)

½ cup sugar, divided

1½ teaspoons active dry yeast

¾ cup lukewarm whole milk (about 80°F)

1 teaspoon pure vanilla extract

2 large eggs

3½ cups (1 pound) unbleached all-purpose flour

1 teaspoon kosher salt

½ cup (1 stick) unsalted butter, at room temperature

This is the master recipe for all the delicious brioche pastries in this chapter. There simply couldn't be a dough more perfect for freshly baked breakfast pastries and afternoon sweets than this one! Brioche dough requires precise mixing, so I prefer to use a stand mixer rather than mix it by hand. Don't be tempted to short the recommended mixing times—brioche's rich, distinctive characteristics depend on careful incorporation of its signature ingredients: eggs, butter, and sugar. To develop even deeper, more complex flavors in your brioche-based pastries, make this dough a day in advance.

MAKES ONE 9-BY-5-INCH LOAF

1. Lightly oil a medium bowl with canola oil. Set aside.

2. In the bowl of a stand mixer fitted with the dough hook, combine the water with 2 teaspoons sugar (taken from the ½ cup sugar). Sprinkle the yeast over the surface of the water. Mix until the yeast is dissolved, then let the mixture sit for 5 minutes to activate the yeast.

3. Add the milk, vanilla, eggs, flour, and salt. Mix on low speed for 3 minutes to bring the dough together, stopping to scrape down the bowl as needed. Increase to medium speed; pinch off grape-size pieces of butter and drop them one at a time into the dough as it mixes (this should take no more than 2 minutes). Continue mixing for 2 to 3 more minutes. Now gradually add the remaining sugar (½ cup minus the 2 teaspoons) and continue mixing for a final 4 minutes. With floured fingers, pinch a big piece of dough and pull it away from the mass. It should stretch about 3 inches without tearing—it will feel a bit like a rubber band. If it tears, mix for another 1 to 3 minutes.

4. Using a rubber spatula, transfer the dough from the bowl onto a floured work surface. Form the dough into a ball and place it in the prepared bowl. Cover with plastic wrap and let the dough rise at room temperature until it has doubled in size, 2½ to 3 hours.

5. Once the dough has risen, you are ready to proceed with any of the recipes in this chapter.

6. If you're making the dough a day ahead—either for convenience or to develop more complex flavors—simply deflate it after its initial rise, then re-cover with plastic wrap and refrigerate overnight. The next day, pull it out 2 hours before you want to use it, and allow it to come to room temperature. The dough should be doubled in size and feel slightly warm to the touch. This dough is best used by the second day. If you'd like to freeze brioche dough, it's best to form it into the desired shape, brush it with egg wash, wrap it well, and freeze for up to a week.

Sugar Buns

Who doesn't love doughnuts? And wouldn't eating a baked *dough-nut make you feel just a little less guilty? These sugar buns are like the best, most beautiful baked doughnuts you've ever come across. They're made with our rich brioche dough, filled with slightly sweetened Mt. Townsend Creamery* fromage blanc, *topped with fresh berries, and dusted in sugar. Could there be a better way to start a day? These are also cute on a breakfast buffet table: simply form half-size buns and bake for about 6 minutes.*

MAKES ONE DOZEN 5-INCH BUNS

1. Line 2 rimmed baking sheets with parchment paper and set aside.

2. Using a rubber spatula, pull the brioche dough onto a floured work surface. Using your hands, flatten and shape the dough into a 7-by-12-inch rectangle. (Do your best to keep the dough an even thickness.) Using a bench knife or plastic scraper, divide the dough into 12 equal pieces by first cutting the rectangle in half lengthwise, then cutting each long piece in half vertically, and finally, cutting each half into 3 pieces.

3. Roll each piece into a 12-inch rope: First roll it into a log, starting with a long side. With both hands held flat over the log, roll back and forth, using a little pressure, until the rope is 12 inches long. Coil the rope (starting from the center and working out), forming a circle that ends up being about 3 inches in diameter. Tuck the ends under. Put 6 buns on each prepared baking sheet, spacing them 2 inches apart—they will expand when proofing. Brush the buns with the egg wash, cover the baking sheets with plastic wrap, and let them rise until they are 4 inches in diameter, about 1 hour at room temperature.

4. Meanwhile, whisk together the fromage blanc, egg, and the 2 table-spoons sugar in a medium bowl. Set aside.

5. About 20 minutes before baking, position 2 racks in the center of the oven and preheat to 375°F.

6. Flatten a 1½-inch circle in the center of a bun and spoon a heaping tablespoon of the cheese mixture into the indentation. Top with 4 or 5 small berries (you may need to quarter large berries such as strawberries). Repeat with the remaining buns. Bake for 10 to 15 minutes, or

1 recipe Sweet Brioche Dough (page 58)

1 large egg beaten with 1 table-spoon water, for egg wash

6 ounces (¾ cup) fromage blanc cheese, preferably from Mt. Townsend Creamery (found at Whole Foods and other specialty markets)

1 large egg

2 tablespoons sugar, plus about ½ cup for topping buns

2 cups fresh seasonal berries

2 tablespoons unsalted butter, melted

until they are deep golden brown. Halfway through baking, rotate the pans to ensure the buns bake evenly. Cool on the baking sheets for 20 minutes.

7. Put the ½ cup sugar in a pie pan. Lightly brush the melted butter on the top and sides of the buns. Roll each bun in the sugar, coating the buttered areas first and then sprinkling a little sugar on the berries.

Cocoa Puffs

Are you a pain au chocolat *fan? You'll experience the same feelings of extreme bliss when eating these puffs; there's just something heavenly about buttery enriched dough combined with warm chocolate. Here, the brioche is formed around a generous dollop of semisweet ganache and then topped with a bittersweet chocolate crackle glaze. These pastries are baked in typical muffin pans, but you'll want to use jumbo-size paper liners, which are 2 inches tall, so that the puffs are the right proportion—then they'll stand out from the crowd in appearance as well as taste.*

MAKES 10 JUMBO-SIZE PASTRIES

1. Distribute 10 jumbo (also called "giant") muffin liners between 2 muffin pans. (Each tray will likely have spaces for 12 muffins.) These pastries bake best when they get full heat circulation, so stagger the liners in each tray to ensure even baking. Set aside.

2. To make the ganache filling, in a small saucepan over medium heat, bring the cream to a froth just before it boils. Turn off the heat and add the chocolate chips, stirring until the chocolate has melted. (If necessary, you can return the mixture to low heat for 1 to 2 minutes.) Pour the ganache into a small bowl and cool to room temperature, about 30 minutes. Ultimately, you want the ganache to be semisolid (so that it will form a ball) but not completely hardened.

3. Meanwhile, using a rubber spatula, pull the brioche dough onto a floured work surface. Flatten and shape it into a 7-by-14-inch rectangle. (Do your best to keep the dough an even thickness.) Using a bench knife or plastic scraper, divide the dough into 10 equal pieces by first cutting the rectangle in half lengthwise, then cutting the halves into 5 equal parts.

4. To make the crackle glaze, in a medium bowl sift the cocoa powder over the sugar and whisk to combine. Add the butter and whisk thoroughly. The glaze is best used when it's warm; reheat it briefly over a double boiler if the butter begins to solidify before you finish forming all the rolls.

FOR THE GANACHE FILLING:

½ cup heavy cream

1 cup good-quality semisweet chocolate chips

1 recipe Sweet Brioche Dough (page 58)

FOR THE CRACKLE GLAZE:

2 tablespoons Dutch-process cocoa powder

½ cup sugar

¼ cup (½ stick) unsalted butter, melted

5. With a 1-inch metal scoop or a spoon, place a heaping teaspoon of ganache in the center of each piece of dough. Gather the dough up around the filling—like a purse with a drawstring—and pinch together the top edges. Dredge the smooth side of the puff in the glaze. Place it, glaze side up, into the prepared muffin pan and continue with the remaining pieces. (This can be a little messy; ideally, you'd like to avoid getting glaze all over the paper liner.) Let the puffs rise for about 1 hour, or until they are level with the tops of the liners.

6. About 20 minutes before baking, position a rack in the center of the oven and preheat to 350°F.

7. Bake for 20 to 25 minutes, or until the puffs' bottoms and sides are golden brown. (If you can't see the color through the liners, it's OK to gently remove one of the puffs from the pan and peel back the paper to check.) Cool in the muffin pans for 20 minutes before serving. While they are best enjoyed the day they are baked, these puffs freeze beautifully—just wrap them securely.

❈ ❈ ❈

VARIATION: NUTELLA PUFFS

Nutella originated in Italy in the 1940s. This smooth, delicious spread has become very popular in the United States. In this variation, we fill our buttery brioche dough with Nutella and finish it with a sprinkle of crunchy turbinado sugar.

To make Nutella Puffs, just substitute Nutella for the chocolate ganache in the Cocoa Puffs. Before baking the rolls, brush the tops lightly with the egg wash, then sprinkle liberally with the sugar. Bake according the directions above.

1½ cups Nutella or other chocolate-hazelnut spread

1 large egg beaten with 1 tablespoon water, for egg wash

¼ cup turbinado sugar

Kugelhopf

Our Kugelhopf starts with rich brioche dough that is laminated with additional butter and layered with a mixture of cinnamon, cocoa, plump currants, and toasted walnuts. Typically this Austrian-inspired coffee cake is enjoyed for breakfast, but warmed and served with a sauce or ice cream, it also makes an outstanding dessert.

MAKES ONE 10-INCH (12-CUP) BUNDT CAKE

1. Flour a rimmed baking sheet and grease a 10-inch Bundt pan with canola oil, making sure to oil all the creases. Set aside.

2. Using a rubber spatula, pull the brioche dough out onto a floured work surface. Using a rolling pin and a dusting of flour, shape the dough into an 8-by-16-inch rectangle, with the long side facing you. (Do your best to keep the dough an even thickness.) Using your fingertips, press the dough, marking it crosswise so it's visually divided into three equal sections.

3. Laminate the dough by layering it with additional butter: With your fingertips, smear the butter pieces on 2 adjacent sections of dough. (If the butter's cold, it won't spread and will tear the dough, so make sure it is sufficiently soft.) Using an offset spatula, spread the butter in an even layer across the 2 sections (see photo #1, page 67).

4. Using your indentations as a guide, fold the unbuttered third onto the center third (see photo #2, page 67). Then fold the far third (with butter) on top (see photo #3, page 67). Even out the edges on all sides and slightly flatten to make the rectangle easier to roll out (see photo #4, page 67). Rotate the dough a quarter turn and roll it out again to an 8-by-16-inch rectangle (see photo #5, page 67). Make the same single fold (this time you will not use butter; just fold the dough into thirds as before; see photo #6, page 67). Transfer the dough to the prepared baking sheet and cover with plastic wrap. Refrigerate for 1 hour to relax the gluten and cool (but not completely chill) the mass of dough and butter.

5. Meanwhile, prepare the filling. Put the currants, vanilla, and hot water in a small bowl. Let sit for 20 minutes; the currants will absorb the flavorful liquid. Drain off any extra liquid and set the plumped currants aside.

1 recipe Sweet Brioche Dough (page 58)

½ cup (1 stick) unsalted butter, cut into quarter-size pieces, at room temperature

1 cup dried currants

2 tablespoons pure vanilla extract

2/3 cup hot water

1 tablespoon plus 1 teaspoon ground cinnamon

1 tablespoon plus 1 teaspoon Dutch-process cocoa powder

1 cup packed dark brown sugar

1⅓ cups (4½ ounces) walnuts, toasted (see Toasting Tips, page 7) and coarsely chopped

½ cup (1 stick) unsalted butter, melted

Confectioners' sugar, for dusting the loaf

6. Combine the cinnamon, cocoa, and brown sugar in a medium bowl. Add the currants, walnuts, and melted butter. Using a rubber spatula, mix well and set aside.

7. Transfer the dough from the baking sheet to a floured work surface. With a rolling pin, roll it out into an 8-by-20-inch rectangle; it should be about ½ inch thick (see photo #7, page 68). With the long side facing you, spread the filling over the dough, leaving a 1-inch border along the edge nearest you (see photo #8, page 68). Starting with the edge farthest away, roll up the dough toward your body (see photo #9, page 68). When you reach the border, stop rolling. Using your fingertips, flatten the dough along the very edge of the border so that it is quite thin—then finish rolling the log. The thin edge acts as a sealer. Let the log rest, seam side down, on your work surface for a few minutes to secure the seal.

8. Flip the log over so the seam side is up and bring the ends together (see photo #10, page 68); join them by tucking one inside the other. Drop this circle of dough into the prepared Bundt pan (see photo #11, page 68). Press the dough down so it fills the pan and any air pockets are deflated (see photo #12, page 68). Check the seam edge: if you notice that the seam is coming apart at any time during the rise, just pinch to reseal. Let the kugelhopf rise at room temperature until the loaf just crests the pan, about 2 hours.

9. About 20 minutes before baking, position a rack in the center of the oven and preheat to 330°F.

10. Bake the loaf for 45 to 50 minutes, or until the top is a deep golden brown. Cool it in the pan for 40 minutes (if turned out right away, it will collapse), then turn it out onto a wire rack to cool completely. Allow the kugelhopf to rest for 1 hour, then dust it with confectioners' sugar, slice with a serrated knife, and serve.

❋ Kugelhopf Steps ❋

The photos below will guide you through each of the important steps you'll be taking when making Kugelhopf. They are not difficult—but on the other hand, they aren't something most of us do every day! The dough is turned and rolled, similar to the technique used when making croissants or puff pastry. I urge you to just plunge into this wonderful recipe—the satiny butter-yellow dough is a pleasure to work with, and the flavors and moist, yet almost flaky texture of the cake translates into a finished product unlike any traditional coffee cake.

1. Flatten dough into an 8-by-16-inch rectangle. Dot butter on two-thirds of the dough; spread evenly with an offset spatula.

2. Place the unbuttered third (far right) onto the center third.

3. Bring the left third of the dough onto the center; this is a single turn.

4. Even out the edges on all sides and slightly flatten to make easier to roll out.

5. Rotate dough one-quarter turn to the right and roll out to 8-by-16 inches.

6. Make one more single turn as you did when enclosing the butter. Cover and refrigerate the dough for 1 hour.

process continued on next page

7. Roll the chilled dough into an 8-by-20-inch rectangle.

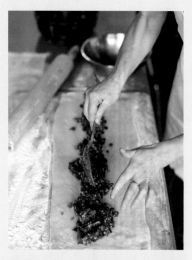

8. Place filling in center of dough and spread it evenly, leaving a 1-inch border along the edge nearest you.

9. Roll the dough toward you, starting from the far edge, moving from left to right.

10. Turn the dough seam side up and tuck one end into the other.

11. Lift the circle of dough into the prepared Bundt pan (still seam side up).

12. Press dough gently into the pan; let rise until it reaches the top of the pan.

Apple Cinnamon Pull-Aparts

The lovely aroma that fills the air when you bake this bread will bring neighbors knocking at your door. Imagine a rich brioche dough rolled up with freshly baked Granny Smith apples and cinnamon sugar; the juices of the apples combine with the sugar to make a decadent glaze. At Macrina we bake the pull-aparts in paper baking molds; I have adapted this recipe to bake in two round 9-inch cake pans. This sweet-but-not-too-sweet bread is perfect for brunch, a picnic, or a midafternoon pick-me-up.

MAKES TWO 9-INCH CAKES

1. Position a rack in the center of the oven and preheat to 350°F. Line a rimmed baking sheet with parchment paper. Lightly grease two round 9-inch cake pans with canola oil. Cut out two 10-inch parchment paper circles and place them in the bottom of the pans, creasing the outer edges so that the paper goes up the sides. Next, cut four 2-inch strips, each 15 inches long, and place along the insides of the pans (2 per pan), slightly overlapping, to ensure the pull-aparts don't stick. Set aside.

2. To make the apples, toss them with the sugar, flour, cinnamon, and nutmeg in a medium bowl. Spread them on the prepared baking sheet and dot with the butter. Bake for 10 minutes, then toss the apples to redistribute them on the baking pan. Bake for another 5 minutes, until the apples are soft to the touch but still a little firm and their juices have thickened somewhat. Cool for 10 minutes, then chop coarsely and set aside.

3. To make the cinnamon sugar, combine the sugars, cinnamon, and vanilla in a medium bowl. Set aside.

4. Using a rubber spatula, pull the brioche dough onto a floured work surface. Using a rolling pin, roll the dough out into an evenly thick 7-by-16-inch rectangle; keep the longer side toward you. Spread the apple filling evenly over the dough, going clear to the edges. Sprinkle the cinnamon sugar over the apples, reserving ¼ cup for garnish.

5. Starting with the edge farthest away, begin rolling up the dough toward you. This dough is fairly soft, so be patient as you are rolling. The log will naturally stretch as you are rolling it, which is good. You want it to stretch to a final length of 24 inches. (Do your best to keep the log the same diameter from one end to the other.) When the log is finished, let it rest seam side down for a few minutes.

FOR THE BAKED APPLES:

3 medium Granny Smith apples, peeled, cored, and sliced ¼ inch thick

¼ cup sugar

1 tablespoon unbleached all-purpose flour

1 teaspoon ground cinnamon

⅛ teaspoon ground nutmeg

2 tablespoons unsalted butter

FOR THE CINNAMON SUGAR:

½ cup granulated sugar

½ cup packed light brown sugar

1½ teaspoons ground cinnamon

1½ teaspoons pure vanilla extract

1 recipe Sweet Brioche Dough (page 58)

1 large egg beaten with 1 teaspoon water, for egg wash

FOR THE BUTTERMILK GLAZE:

2 cups confectioners' sugar

1 teaspoon pure vanilla extract

2 to 3 tablespoons buttermilk

6. Halve the log so you have two 12-inch-long logs. Then cut each log into seven 1½-inch pieces—they'll resemble cinnamon rolls. Set 6 pieces on end around the perimeter of one prepared pan, then place the last one in the center. Make sure they are evenly spaced—they will need room to rise. Do the same with the second pan. Lightly brush the egg wash on top, and sprinkle with the reserved cinnamon sugar. Let the dough rise until it's level with the top of the pan and has expanded to fill it, about 1½ hours.

7. About 20 minutes before baking, position a rack in the center of the oven and preheat to 325°F.

8. Bake the pull-aparts for 30 to 35 minutes, or until they are golden brown. Cool them in the pan for just 20 minutes (don't let them cool completely, as the sugars will set up and stick). Flip the rolls onto a plate and remove the parchment paper. Then place your presentation plate on top of the rolls and flip again, presenting them right side up.

9. Make the buttermilk glaze by sifting the sugar into a medium bowl. Add the vanilla and buttermilk and whisk to remove any lumps. Stream the glaze over the top of the pull-aparts in a zigzag pattern. (I think this gives the bread a better look and a more balanced taste than simply covering the whole top with glaze.) Serve warm.

10. Since this recipe makes 2 pans, you can freeze one and have it ready for impromptu company or Sunday brunch with your family: wait until the glaze has hardened, then wrap the entire pull-apart in plastic wrap and freeze for up to 4 weeks. To serve, remove from the freezer and let the pull-aparts thaw at room temperature for 2 hours. Preheat the oven to 325°F. Place the pull-aparts on a parchment paper–lined baking sheet and reheat for 10 minutes.

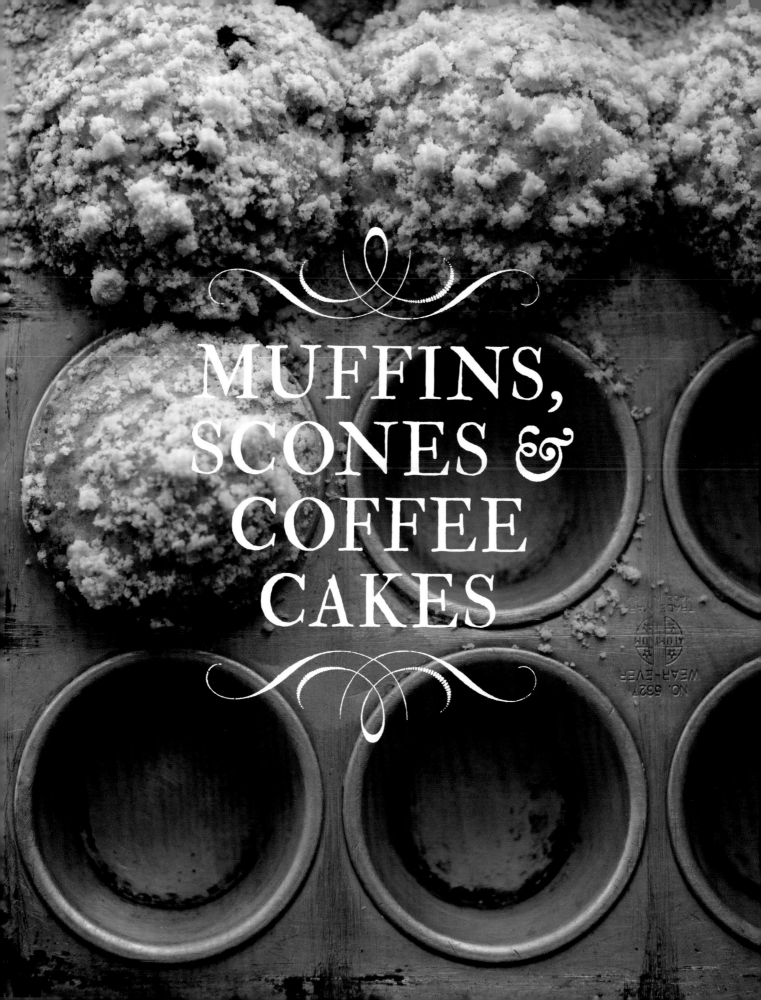

MUFFINS, SCONES & COFFEE CAKES

MY GREATEST "GET UP AND GO" motivator for my thirteen-year-old daughter Olivia is the promise of a fresh-baked buttermilk biscuit with strawberry jam, still warm from the oven at one of our cafés. Seriously—who would miss the chance to choose from a gorgeous display of fresh muffins, scones, croissant- and brioche-based pastries, and coffee cakes (not to mention inhaling their irresistible aromas)?

It's our loyal customers who drive the development of so many of our products; they love our ever-changing selection and look forward to the next seasonal offerings. This chapter features some of those treats, such as our tender Summer Berry Muffins with Corn Flour and cakelike Cranberry Gingerbread Muffins topped with cream cheese frosting. If you're looking for scones, this chapter offers an airy, fresh Blueberry-Orange Cream Scone; a moist but not overly sweet Vegan Pumpkin Spice Scone; and a tasty, light-textured, Gluten-Free Oat Flour and Blackberry Jelly Biscuit—all developed from customer requests.

Probably the most sought-after recipe in this entire book is our Orange–Chocolate Chip Coffee Cake with a chocolate glaze; it was featured on television's *Unique Sweets* cooking series several years back. This coffee cake is ever so moist and fragrant as it's made with a generous amount of sour cream and butter, then layered with essences of fresh orange juice and zest, toasted almonds, and chocolate.

Most of these recipes can be simply mixed together by hand: use a rubber spatula to fold the sifted dry ingredients into the wet and mix gently just until most of the dry ingredients are incorporated. Likewise, when a recipe calls for cutting butter into the dry ingredients, use a light hand—excessive mixing will deflate the batter and toughen your finished product. One last tip: Sifting the dry ingredients (brown sugar included) may take a bit more time, but it's worth the trouble—you'll end up with a finer-textured finished product that's worthy of your efforts.

Whether you bake these breakfast treats at home or entice your friends to meet you in front of one of Macrina's overflowing pastry cases, there's no better reason to get up and go than the promise of one of these delicious pastries.

Summer Berry Muffins with Corn Flour

Corn flour delivers the delicious, sweet flavor of cornmeal but has a more refined texture. If you can't find corn flour, medium-ground cornmeal will work—the texture will just be a little crunchy. This muffin combines the perfect balance of white and brown sugars with lemon zest and a hint of vanilla, blended nicely with sweet summer berries and finished with a streusel topping. This is truly my favorite muffin!

MAKES 10 STANDARD-SIZE MUFFINS

1. Position a rack in the center of the oven and preheat to 350°F. Grease the top of a standard-size muffin pan with canola oil and line 10 cups with paper liners. Set aside.

2. To make the streusel topping, combine the flours and sugar in a medium bowl. Cut the butter into the flour mixture with a fork or pastry cutter until the mixture has a coarse, crumbly texture. Add the almond extract and mix for another 30 seconds. Set aside.

3. To make the batter, sift together the flours, granulated and brown sugars, baking powder, and salt in a medium bowl. Add the lemon zest and mix well. Whisk together the eggs, milk, and vanilla in a separate medium bowl.

4. Working quickly and gently with a rubber spatula (overmixing can result in tough muffins), fold the egg mixture into the dry ingredients in 3 additions. With the last addition, add the berries. Give the batter two strokes with the spatula to just fold in the berries. Add the melted butter by pouring it in a stream, creating a circle on the top of the batter. Continue to fold gently until the butter is just incorporated (some of the dry ingredients may not be fully absorbed). Let the batter sit for 4 minutes before dividing; it will thicken up and be easier to scoop.

5. Divide the batter among 10 muffin cups, filling them to the top of the liner, heaping the batter slightly. Sprinkle each muffin generously with streusel topping. Bake for 30 minutes, or until the muffins are golden brown on top and a skewer inserted into the center comes out

FOR THE STREUSEL TOPPING:

⅓ cup unbleached all-purpose flour

2 tablespoons corn flour or medium-ground cornmeal

¼ cup sugar

2 tablespoons chilled unsalted butter, cut into ¼-inch pieces

⅛ teaspoon pure almond extract

FOR THE BATTER:

1¾ cups unbleached all-purpose flour

½ cup plus 2 tablespoons corn flour or medium-ground cornmeal

¼ cup plus 3 tablespoons granulated sugar

½ cup packed light brown sugar

1 tablespoon baking powder

¾ teaspoon kosher salt

1½ teaspoons lemon zest (from about 1 large lemon)

3 large eggs

1 cup plus 2 tablespoons whole milk

1½ teaspoons pure vanilla extract

1½ cups assorted fresh berries, large berries halved or quartered

6 tablespoons (¾ stick) unsalted butter, melted

clean. Cool in the pan for 20 minutes, then transfer to a wire rack to cool completely.

6. While these are best eaten the day they are baked, like most muffins and scones, you can also wrap them securely and freeze for up to 2 weeks. To serve, thaw them and reheat in a 325°F oven for about 8 minutes.

Vegan Banana Ginger Muffins

More and more, customers are requesting low-fat and vegan items from our pastry cases. As we've perfected this muffin recipe over the years, we've learned that freshly grated ginger and pureed bananas give the muffins a big hit of bold flavor and extra moistness. The nourishing whole wheat flour, combined with toasted walnuts, fresh orange juice, and agave syrup, add up to a flavorful, healthy breakfast treat. We always aim to please!

MAKES 8 STANDARD-SIZE MUFFINS

1. Position a rack in the center of the oven and preheat to 350°F. Grease the top of a standard-size muffin pan with canola oil and line 8 cups with paper liners. Set aside.

2. Sift together the flours, baking powder, baking soda, egg substitute, and salt in a medium bowl. Add the walnuts and mix well. In a food processor or blender, puree the bananas until very smooth. Transfer the puree to a separate medium bowl, and add the fresh ginger, lemon zest, agave syrup, orange juice, canola oil, and vanilla. Whisk to thoroughly combine.

3. Working quickly and gently with a rubber spatula (overmixing can result in tough muffins), fold the banana mixture into the dry ingredients in 2 additions. Continue to fold until all the flour is moistened (the batter may still be a little lumpy).

4. Divide the batter among 8 muffin cups, filling them to the top of the liner and heaping the batter slightly. (I use an ice cream scoop for this job; it helps direct the batter into the cup rather than all over the top of the tin. You may also find that a ⅓ cup measure with a handle works well.) Top each muffin with a piece of candied ginger and a sprinkle of turbinado sugar. Bake for 30 minutes, or until the muffins are golden brown on top and a skewer inserted into the center comes out clean. Cool in the pan for 20 minutes, then transfer to a wire rack to cool completely.

1¼ cups unbleached all-purpose flour

¾ cup stone-ground whole wheat flour

1½ teaspoons baking powder

1 teaspoon baking soda

2 teaspoons egg replacement powder (see page xxv)

1 teaspoon kosher salt

1 cup walnut halves and pieces, toasted (see Toasting Tips, page 7) and coarsely chopped

2 ripe medium bananas

2 teaspoons peeled, grated fresh ginger

2 teaspoons lemon zest (from about 1 large lemon)

⅓ cup amber agave syrup

¾ cup freshly squeezed orange juice (from about 2 large oranges)

⅓ cup canola oil

1 tablespoon pure vanilla extract

4 small pieces candied ginger, cut in half at an angle, for garnish

¼ cup turbinado sugar, for garnish

❖ *The* INTERNATIONAL CULTURE *of* MACRINA ❖

It's morning at Macrina, and the heat is already building in the small space where five or six people work side by side, chatting and often smiling—but always working dexterously and very, very hard. These folks are part of our small army of wholesale pastry bakers; they work in several shifts to craft the abundance of scones, biscuits, cookies, muffins, and coffee cakes that go out each and every day to our wholesale customers: local grocery stores, cafés, a nearby hospital, caterers, and many restaurants throughout the Seattle area. What makes this team different is that they're mostly of Vietnamese descent—ranging in age from their mid-twenties to mid-sixties—and what makes them shine is the quality of their work and their incredible work ethic.

Take Thuc Nguyen—a forward-thinking, sixty-year-old mother of two who immigrated to the United States about twelve years ago. Or Tramy Le, who came at a much younger age and has grown into a skilled baker, as well as Macrina's liaison, bridging baking and language skills with the pastry staff. Each has worked with Macrina for more than ten years.

Thuc was a schoolteacher in post-war Vietnam, and later ran a grocery store with her husband while raising their two daughters. Her political views were not popular ones, and she and her family fled to Seattle for the freedoms it promised. She had a lot to learn when she was hired as a bread baker at Macrina, but she dove into it with all her might. Thuc spoke very little English (she is still learning and is an avid student in the ESL courses offered by our company); her strategy for learning the new craft was to memorize the dough-forming sequence and the different shapes made from each variety. She kept a notebook that she studied every night until it was committed to memory and she could pronounce the names of the products. Later she moved to the pastry department and started all over. Learning tablespoons, ounces, currants, apricots, creaming, and whipping to stiff peaks—it was all just gibberish at the beginning! But her determination was unstoppable, and that spirit makes her one of our best.

Tramy Le was twenty-eight when she moved to Seattle. She and her husband had met at a Tet (Lunar New Year) celebration in Ho Chi Minh City, and decided to forge a new life for themselves in America. Tramy had studied English in high school and at a university, so she had the advantage of being able to read recipes and instructions—but understanding and participating in English conversations was intimidating for a long while. Her work stood out, and she has risen steadily through the ranks. She's now assistant manager for Macrina's wholesale pastry team, a job that fully utilizes her pastry and organizational skills. And her continuing role as translator for her Vietnamese staff provides a bridge to understanding that we've all come to depend on greatly.

These two "pastry ladies" (as everyone affectionately calls them) and their whole pastry team are such an important part of the big picture at Macrina. Their products contribute about 30 percent of our daily wholesale revenues! No business owner could miss that fact, seeing the racks of freshly glazed pastries waiting to be delivered each morning. It's a win-win situation: Thuc and Tramy have learned to function at a high level in a new culture, and we at Macrina gain inspiration and energy from their dedication and pride of craft.

Brown Sugar–Oatmeal "Sunshine" Muffins

FOR THE CINNAMON-SUGAR TOPPING:

2 tablespoons granulated sugar

2 tablespoons light brown sugar

½ teaspoon ground cinnamon

⅛ teaspoon ground nutmeg

FOR THE BATTER:

1 cup packed light brown sugar

1 cup unbleached all-purpose flour

¼ cup whole wheat flour

1 tablespoon baking powder

½ teaspoon ground cinnamon

⅛ teaspoon ground nutmeg

½ teaspoon kosher salt

½ cup plus 2 tablespoons thick-cut rolled oats, divided

¾ cup buttermilk

1½ teaspoons pure vanilla extract

2 large eggs

¼ cup (½ stick) unsalted butter, melted and cooled

1 heaping cup (about ¾ pint) fresh raspberries

Here in rainy Seattle we celebrate that bright, warm sun in the sky any chance we get! But even on a wet day, these tasty muffins will bring a smile to your face and a positive change in your mood. They bake with lovely caramel tones from the brown sugar and a nice contrast from fresh, seasonal raspberries. (Feel free to substitute individually quick-frozen raspberries if fresh are not available.) Add a little sunshine to your day!

MAKES 8 STANDARD-SIZE MUFFINS

1. Position a rack in the center of the oven and preheat to 335°F. Grease the top of a standard-size muffin pan with canola oil so the muffin tops don't stick and line 8 cups with paper liners. Set aside.

2. To make the cinnamon-sugar topping, whisk or rub together with your fingertips the granulated and brown sugars, cinnamon, and nutmeg in a small bowl until thoroughly distributed. Set aside.

3. To make the batter, sift together the brown sugar, flours, baking powder, cinnamon, nutmeg, and salt in a medium bowl. Add the ½ cup oats and whisk to thoroughly combine. Whisk together the buttermilk, vanilla, and eggs in a separate medium bowl.

4. Make a well in the center of the dry ingredients, then pour the buttermilk mixture into the center. Working quickly and gently (overmixing can result in tough muffins), fold the dry ingredients into the wet by making just 3 passes with a rubber spatula. Add the melted butter by pouring it in a stream, creating a circle on the top of the batter. Continue to fold until the butter is just incorporated (some of the dry ingredients may not be fully absorbed), then gently fold in the raspberries.

5. Divide the batter among 8 muffin cups. (I use an ice cream scoop—it makes this job a breeze.) The batter will be slightly mounded. Top the muffins with the remaining 2 tablespoons oats and a dusting of cinnamon-sugar topping. Bake for 25 to 30 minutes, or until the muffins are golden brown on top and a skewer inserted into the center comes out clean. Cool for about 20 minutes in the pan, then transfer to a wire rack to cool completely.

Cranberry Gingerbread Muffins

These muffins are so delectable and tender, you could almost call them cakes. The buttery, sweet molasses batter is loaded with brown sugar, fresh grated ginger, and dried cranberries, then the muffins are topped with a slightly sweetened cream cheese frosting. They make excellent tea cakes or individual desserts for any fall gathering.

MAKES 8 STANDARD-SIZE MUFFINS

1. Position a rack in the center of the oven and preheat to 325°F. Grease the top of a standard-size muffin pan with canola oil and line 8 cups with paper liners. Set aside.

2. To make the batter, soak ¼ cup of the cranberries in a small bowl filled with hot water to cover for 20 minutes. Drain off any excess water and set the plumped cranberries aside.

3. Sift together the flour, baking powder, baking soda, and salt in a medium bowl and set aside.

4. In the bowl of a stand mixer fitted with the paddle attachment or in a large bowl using an electric mixer, mix the butter, brown sugar, and ginger on medium speed for 5 minutes, or until very fluffy and pale. Scrape down the sides of the bowl with a rubber spatula as needed to ensure that the ingredients are well incorporated.

5. Add the egg to the butter mixture and mix on low speed until fully incorporated. Add the egg yolk and ¼ cup of the dry ingredients and mix on low for 30 seconds. With the mixer running, drizzle the molasses into the bowl near the edge. When it is well distributed, stop the mixer and scrape down the sides of the bowl.

6. Remove the bowl from the mixer. Working quickly and gently with a rubber spatula (overmixing can result in tough muffins), fold in the remaining dry ingredients in 3 parts, alternating with the buttermilk in 2 parts. On the last addition of the dry mixture, add the plumped cranberries.

7. Divide the batter among 8 muffin cups. The batter will be slightly mounded. Bake for 25 to 30 minutes, or until the muffins are deep golden brown on top and a skewer inserted into the center comes out

FOR THE BATTER:

¼ cup dried cranberries, plus 8 more for garnish

1½ cups unbleached all-purpose flour

¾ teaspoon baking powder

¾ teaspoon baking soda

¼ teaspoon kosher salt

½ cup (1 stick) unsalted butter, at room temperature

⅓ cup packed light brown sugar

1 tablespoon peeled, grated fresh ginger

1 large egg

1 large egg yolk

½ cup dark molasses, preferably blackstrap

¾ cup buttermilk

FOR THE FROSTING:

5 ounces cream cheese, at room temperature

6 tablespoons (¾ stick) unsalted butter, at room temperature

¾ cup confectioners' sugar, sifted

¼ cup whole milk

clean. Cool in the pan for 20 minutes, then transfer to a wire rack to cool completely before frosting.

8. To make the frosting, in the bowl of a stand mixer fitted with the paddle attachment, mix the cream cheese and butter on medium speed until smooth. Add the confectioners' sugar and continue mixing until no lumps remain, scraping down the sides of the bowl occasionally. Gradually add the milk and mix until the frosting is spreadable.

9. I use a small (#30) ice cream scoop to top the muffins with frosting. Simply drop the frosting on the muffin and, with an offset spatula, spread the frosting almost to the edges. Frost the muffins and garnish with the remaining 8 dried cranberries.

NOTE: You can easily dress up this muffin by making sugared fresh cranberries and sugared fresh bay leaves. Lightly brush the cranberries and bay leaves with pasteurized egg whites and then roll or dip them in granulated sugar. Let them dry on a wire rack for about 1 hour. Dust each muffin with decorating sugar (a coarse crystallized sugar also called sanding sugar, found in most major supermarkets), then place a few cranberries and bay leaves on top for a beautiful, sparkly garnish.

Blueberry-Orange Cream Scones

Cream scones are the cream of the crop. While most scone recipes use butter or heavy cream in the dough, we use a different technique: we whip the cream and then fold it into the dry ingredients. This aerates the scones during the baking process much as butter does and gives them an especially light, delicate texture—making jam almost unnecessary!

MAKES SIX 4½-INCH SCONES

¾ cup heavy cream

1½ cups unbleached all-purpose flour

⅓ cup plus 1 tablespoon sugar

1 tablespoon baking powder

½ teaspoon kosher salt

1 tablespoon orange zest (from 1 medium orange)

1¼ cups fresh blueberries

⅓ cup buttermilk

1 large egg beaten with 1 teaspoon water, for egg wash

¼ cup sugar, for garnish

1. Line a rimmed baking sheet with parchment paper and set aside.

2. With a hand mixer or a whisk, whip the heavy cream in a medium bowl until it forms medium-soft peaks. Sift together the flour, sugar, baking powder, and salt in a separate medium bowl. Mix in the orange zest with your fingers until evenly distributed.

3. Working quickly and gently with a rubber spatula (overmixing can result in tough scones), fold the dry ingredients into the whipped cream in 3 additions. On the last addition, add the blueberries and the buttermilk. Continue folding quickly until the buttermilk is evenly distributed and the flour is just incorporated.

4. Turn the dough out onto a floured work surface and shape into a 3-by-12-inch rectangle about 1 inch thick. Cut the dough crosswise into 3 equal squares, then cut diagonally through each square to make a total of 6 triangle-shaped scones. (You can make the scones in many different sizes and shapes; just adjust the baking time by keeping a close eye on their color.) Place the scones on the prepared baking sheet, spacing them about 2 inches apart; they will expand during baking. Transfer the pan to the freezer for 30 minutes. (Chilling the dough will help the scones keep their shape while baking.)

5. Meanwhile, position a rack in the center of the oven and preheat to 375°F.

6. Lightly brush the egg wash over the scones and sprinkle them generously with sugar. Bake for 25 to 30 minutes, or until the scones are golden brown on the top and bottom. Cool on the pan for 20 minutes, then transfer to a wire rack to cool completely.

Vegan Pumpkin Spice Scones

½ cup golden raisins

1¼ cups unbleached all-purpose flour

½ cup tapioca flour

½ cup white vegan sugar

1 tablespoon baking powder

¼ teaspoon ground cinnamon

½ teaspoon kosher salt

2 teaspoons peeled, grated fresh ginger

⅓ cup raw pumpkin seeds, toasted (see Toasting Tips, page 7) and coarsely chopped

¼ cup (½ stick) chilled vegan butter (preferably Earth Balance Vegan Buttery Sticks), cut into pea-size pieces

1 cup pumpkin puree

¼ cup freshly squeezed orange juice (from about 1 large orange)

¼ cup turbinado sugar, for garnish

The lively autumn flavors of pumpkin puree, ground cinnamon, and fresh ginger are front and center in this moist and flavorful vegan scone. Vegan diets are composed of plant-based ingredients, thus ruling out all animal products as well as any ingredients processed using animal products. Obvious exclusions are meat, fish, eggs, and milk. Less obvious are honey and even cane sugar, which is unacceptable because it goes through a final purification process using a filter made of animal bone char. When you're shopping for sugar that is vegan, first look for beet sugar (available in most major grocery stores), which is exempt from this filtering process.

MAKES SIX 4½-INCH SCONES

1. Position a rack in the center of the oven and preheat to 350°F. Line a rimmed baking sheet with parchment paper and set aside. Fill a spray bottle with water and set aside.

2. Soak the raisins in a small bowl filled with hot water to cover for 20 minutes. Drain off any excess water and set the plumped raisins aside.

3. Sift together the flours, sugar, baking powder, cinnamon, and salt in a medium bowl. Mix in the ginger with your fingers until evenly distributed.

4. Add the pumpkin seeds to the dry ingredients and mix briefly to distribute. Cut in the butter with a pastry cutter or two forks until the mixture is coarse and crumbly. Using a rubber spatula, stir in the pumpkin puree, raisins, and orange juice and mix until just combined; make sure all the bits on the sides and bottom of the bowl are incorporated. (The less you mix, the more tender the scones will be.)

5. Turn the dough out onto a floured work surface and pat it into a 4-by-9-inch rectangle about 1 inch thick. Cut the dough crosswise into 3 equal squares, then cut diagonally through each square to make a total of 6 triangle-shaped scones. Place the scones 2 inches apart on the prepared baking sheet. Using the spray bottle, mist the top of the scones with water and then sprinkle them with the turbinado sugar. Bake for 30 to 35 minutes, or until the scones are golden brown on the top and bottom. Cool on the sheet for 20 minutes, then transfer to a wire rack to cool completely.

Gluten-Free Oat Flour and Blackberry Jelly Biscuits

These delicious, lightly sweetened gluten-free biscuits are made with flavorful, nutritious flours ground from oats, tapioca, and brown rice. With the absence of gluten in the flours, you'll need to add a bit of powdered xanthan gum (made from fermented corn syrup and found in the specialty flour sections of most stores), which binds and adds volume to baked products. Without the xanthan gum, the biscuits would be quite crumbly. Some gluten-intolerant individuals are also sensitive to oat flour (oats contain a protein similar to gluten); for those folks, you may substitute gluten-free oat flour or sweet white sorghum flour. Each biscuit is loaded with a generous scoop of jelly, so you get blackberry with every bite!

MAKES EIGHT 4-INCH BISCUITS

1. Position a rack in the center of the oven and preheat to 350°F. Line a rimmed baking sheet with parchment paper.

2. Sift together the flours, ¼ cup of the sugar, xanthan gum, baking powder, and salt in a medium bowl and whisk thoroughly to combine. Make a well in the center and pour in 2 cups of the cream. Working quickly and gently with a rubber spatula (overmixing can result in tough scones), fold the cream into the dry ingredients. This should take about 1 minute.

3. Sprinkle a work surface with brown rice flour. Turn the dough out and roll it into a 3-by-14-inch log. Divide the log in half, then cut each half into 4 pieces to make a total of 8 equal pieces. Form each piece into a roughly circle-shaped biscuit. Place the biscuits 2 inches apart on the prepared baking sheet. Brush the tops of the biscuits with the remaining 2 tablespoons cream and sprinkle them with the remaining ¼ cup sugar. Bake for 25 to 30 minutes, or until the biscuits are golden brown on the top and bottom. Cool on the sheet for 15 minutes.

4. Using a teaspoon, scoop out a quarter-size piece from the center of each biscuit, digging about halfway down. Fill each indentation with about 1 tablespoon of the blackberry jelly.

1 cup brown rice flour

1 cup tapioca flour

¾ cup oat flour

½ cup sugar, divided

1½ teaspoons xanthan gum

1 tablespoon plus ½ teaspoon baking powder

½ teaspoon kosher salt

2 cups plus 2 tablespoons heavy cream, divided

½ cup good-quality blackberry jelly or other fruit jelly or jam

Budapest Coffee Cake with Sweetened Tart Cherries

FOR THE FILLING:

½ cup dried sweetened tart cherries, coarsely chopped (for a more traditional coffee cake, use dried currants or raisins)

½ cup packed light brown sugar

2 teaspoons ground cinnamon

2 teaspoons Dutch-process cocoa powder

⅔ cup walnuts, toasted (see Toasting Tips, page 7) and coarsely chopped

FOR THE BATTER:

3 cups unbleached all-purpose flour

1½ teaspoons baking powder

1½ teaspoons baking soda

½ teaspoon kosher salt

¾ cup (1½ sticks) unsalted butter, at room temperature

1½ cups granulated sugar

2 tablespoons pure vanilla extract

3 large eggs

2 cups low-fat yogurt

We opened our doors in 1993 with this coffee cake perched on a glass pedestal on top of our pastry case. Its flavors follow the lines of a traditional sour cream coffee cake, but I use low-fat yogurt in place of sour cream to make it lighter and more suitable for breakfast. To celebrate our bountiful local ingredients, I've added plumped, sweetened tart cherries (also known as pie cherries) from Chukar Cherries, a long-established, family-run business located in Eastern Washington wine country. (Chukar Cherries are available online, or use dried currants or raisins for a more traditional substitute.) These tasty, crimson bites add a wonderful complexity of flavor, color, and texture to the layers of cocoa powder and cinnamon sugar. I like to garnish this lovely coffee cake with a dusting of confectioners' sugar and a bouquet of garden flowers in the center.

MAKES ONE 10-INCH (12-CUP) BUNDT CAKE

1. Position a rack in the center of the oven and preheat to 325°F. Grease a 10-inch Bundt pan with canola oil, making sure to oil all the creases. Set aside.

2. To make the filling, soak the cherries in a small bowl filled with hot water to cover for 20 minutes. Drain off any excess water and set the plumped cherries aside.

3. Mix together the brown sugar, cinnamon, and cocoa powder in a medium bowl, breaking up any lumps. Add the walnuts and cherries. Using your hands, toss to evenly distribute the ingredients. Set aside.

4. To make the batter, sift together the flour, baking powder, baking soda, and salt in a medium-size bowl. Set aside.

5. In the bowl of a stand mixer fitted with the paddle attachment or in a large bowl using an electric mixer, cream the butter and granulated sugar. Start on low speed and gradually increase to medium, for a total of 5 to 8 minutes, until the mixture becomes light and pale. Using a rubber spatula, scrape down the bowl as needed in order to fully incorporate the ingredients. On low speed add the vanilla and then the eggs, one at a time, making sure to fully incorporate each egg before

adding the next. Scrape down the bowl again. Working quickly and gently (overmixing can result in a tough cake), add the flour mixture in 3 additions alternating with the yogurt in 2 additions. I like to mix the batter until it's almost smooth, then remove the bowl and finish up with a few strokes of the spatula.

6. Begin layering the batter into the prepared Bundt pan: you'll use 3 layers of batter and 2 layers of filling (plus a final sprinkle of filling on top to garnish). Start by filling the base of the pan with one-third of the batter; flatten and smooth the layer using a small offset spatula or the back of a spoon. Sprinkle with ⅓ cup of filling. (It's best to keep the filling away from the edge of the pan since the sugary mixture tends to stick.) Add the second third of the batter and smooth evenly, then add another ⅓ cup of filling. Top with the remaining batter, smoothing it to the edges of the pan. Garnish with the remaining filling, sprinkling it evenly over the top.

7. Bake for 50 to 55 minutes, or until the cake is deep golden brown on top and a skewer inserted into the center comes out clean. Cool in the pan for 1 hour, then turn the cake out of the pan onto a plate.

Orange–Chocolate Chip Coffee Cake

This coffee cake was featured on the Cooking Channel's Unique Sweets *series, which showcases eateries across the United States that are creating "the most unique and exciting desserts today." This moist, buttery cake is studded with roasted almonds, semisweet chocolate chips, and fresh orange zest—it looks incredibly intoxicating on camera! We've gotten calls from people all across the country wanting this recipe. Here it is for you.*

NOTE: For convenience, this version makes two standard-size loaf cakes; you can use a 10-inch Bundt pan for a fancier presentation. The baking time will be close to 1 hour.

MAKES TWO 4½-BY-8-INCH LOAF CAKES

1. Position a rack in the center of the oven and preheat to 325°F. Grease two 4½-by-8-inch loaf pans with canola oil and set aside.

2. To make the batter, sift together the flour, sugar, baking powder, baking soda, and salt in a medium bowl. Mix in the orange zest with your fingers until evenly distributed. Set aside.

3. Whisk together the orange juice, vanilla, eggs, and ¼ cup of the sour cream in a separate medium bowl until thoroughly combined. Set aside.

4. In the bowl of a stand mixer fitted with the paddle attachment, mix the dry ingredients, ½ cup of the almonds, and the chocolate chips on low speed. Add the butter pieces a few at a time, beating on low speed until smooth and stopping to scrape the sides of the bowl as necessary. Add the remaining ¾ cup sour cream. Mix for about 1 minute on low speed, until the mixture becomes a paste, stopping to scrape the sides of the bowl to ensure all the ingredients are incorporated. Add the egg mixture in 3 additions, mixing for 20 seconds each time. Scrape down the bowl after each addition to help prevent overmixing, which can toughen the cake.

5. Divide the batter between the two loaf pans, filling them about two-thirds full, and smooth the tops with a small offset spatula or the back of a spoon. Bake for 45 to 50 minutes, or until the cakes are golden brown on top and a skewer inserted into the center comes out clean.

FOR THE BATTER:

1¾ cups unbleached all-purpose flour

1 cup sugar

1½ teaspoons baking powder

1 teaspoon baking soda

½ teaspoon kosher salt

Zest of 2 medium oranges (about 2 tablespoons)

1 tablespoon freshly squeezed orange juice

1½ teaspoons pure vanilla extract

3 large eggs

1 cup sour cream, divided

¾ cup raw almonds (skins on), toasted (see Toasting Tips, page 7) and coarsely chopped, divided

1 cup semisweet chocolate chips

2 sticks (1 cup) unsalted butter, each cut into thirds, at room temperature

FOR THE ORANGE SYRUP:

½ cup sugar

⅓ cup fresh orange juice (squeezed from the zested oranges)

FOR THE CHOCOLATE GLAZE:

¾ cup heavy cream

¾ cup semisweet chocolate chips

Cool the cakes in the pan for 20 minutes, then turn them out onto a plate. Poke about 20 holes in the top of each of the loaves with a skewer.

6. To make the orange syrup, heat the sugar and orange juice in a medium saucepan. Cook for 3 to 5 minutes over medium heat, stirring constantly, until the mixture becomes a clear syrup. Brush the hot syrup on the tops of the loaves. Do this several times, using all the syrup. Cool the cakes for 30 minutes while you make the chocolate glaze.

7. To make the chocolate glaze, in a small saucepan over medium heat, bring the cream to a froth just before it boils, watching it carefully so it doesn't boil over. Remove the pan from the heat and add the chocolate chips. Using a whisk, combine the cream and chocolate; they will melt into a smooth glaze. Dip a spoon into the glaze and streak the top of each cake in a tight zigzag pattern. While the chocolate is still warm, sprinkle the remaining $\frac{1}{4}$ cup almonds down the centers of the loaves.

Apple and Brandied-Prune Coffee Cake

This coffee cake reminds me of a breakfast offering you'd get in Normandy, France, because it contains the classic combination of apples, brandy-soaked prunes, and roasted sweet walnuts. It makes its appearance at Macrina around Christmas each year. Cousin to the traditional fruitcake, it has a much lighter texture and requires far less of a time commitment to make. The plentiful amount of apples and prunes in this recipe creates a very moist coffee cake, which intensifies in flavor on the second and third days. Instead of losing its fresh qualities with time as so many baked goods do, this one actually improves. I'd originally planned to substitute vanilla for the brandy (this is, after all, a breakfast item), but when I did, the magic was gone. So live it up!

MAKES ONE 9-INCH ROUND CAKE

1. Position a rack in the center of the oven and preheat to 325°F. Grease a 9-inch Pyrex pan or 1½-inch-deep ceramic baking dish with canola oil. You'll serve this cake directly from the baking dish, so use the prettiest dish you have.

2. In a medium bowl, soak the prunes in the brandy for at least 20 minutes, stirring once or twice.

3. In a medium bowl, sift together the flour, cinnamon, baking soda, and salt. Add the lemon zest and walnuts and toss to combine, making sure the zest is well distributed.

4. Toss the apples with the sugar in a medium bowl until thoroughly coated, then pour the butter over the mixture and stir to coat. Whisk the egg in a small bowl and add to the apple mixture, then add the prunes with any leftover brandy and stir for another 30 seconds. Working quickly and gently (overmixing can result in a tough cake), fold in the dry ingredients in 3 additions.

5. Pour the batter into the prepared pan and smooth the top with a small offset spatula or the back of a spoon. Bake for 1 hour, or until the top and bottom of the cake are deep brown and a skewer inserted into the center comes out clean.

6. Cool the cake in the pan for 45 minutes, then dust with the confectioners' sugar.

¾ cup dried prunes, cut into thirds

2 tablespoons brandy

1¼ cups unbleached all-purpose flour

1 teaspoon ground cinnamon

1 teaspoon baking soda

½ teaspoon kosher salt

1 teaspoon lemon zest

⅔ cup walnuts, toasted (see Toasting Tips, page 7) and coarsely chopped

2 medium Granny Smith apples, peeled, cored, and diced into ½-inch pieces

1 cup sugar

½ cup (1 stick) unsalted butter, melted and cooled

1 large egg

2 tablespoons confectioners' sugar, for garnish

COOKIES

IF YOU'RE LOOKING FOR A universal expression of kindness, heartfelt thanks, or "things will get better soon," you've come to the right place. Cookies say it all, in the most unpretentious way—after all, weren't cookies the first things we baked as kids? Since then, we've learned that even the humble cookie can be sophisticated and full of complex flavors and textures. With only a few everyday ingredients, we can enjoy baking—and take pleasure in sharing—marvelous, put-a-smile-on-your-face cookies.

Simple as cookies are, you do need to follow a few baking guidelines that will reward you with consistently great results. Thoroughly creaming the butter and sugar will add lightness to your cookies and allow them to spread nicely during baking. If possible, bring your eggs to room temperature before adding; they'll blend more easily into the creamed butter mixture. When adding the flour and leavening, you'll want to just combine the ingredients; overmixing will develop the gluten in the flour and make the cookies tough. On that note, completely cool your cookie dough before baking—it will take about two hours to chill the fats and relax the glutens. Make sure your oven is preheated to the proper temperature and your cookie dough is slightly cool when it goes in the oven, since warm cookie dough will spread excessively. For ease of portioning, I use a small ice cream scoop. Push the dough into the scoop and flatten the top: the cookies will bake evenly and be a uniform size—plus, there will be a flat surface to keep the dough in place on the baking sheet. You now are ready to bake some scrumptious cookies!

I've packed this chapter with ten special recipes. Many are old-fashioned favorites with a modern twist, such as the Oatmeal Apricot Pecan Cookies, Car-co-doodles, and a vegan Tollhouse-like chocolate chip cookie. For great gift giving, we offer two shortbread recipes: the elegant Pistachio and the rich Chocolate Hazelnut. Another standout is a gluten-free Chocolate Melt, thin and crispy on the edges and soft in the center. And there are more, so go ahead—browse through the chapter and find your new favorite.

Oatmeal Apricot Pecan Cookies

1 cup unbleached all-purpose flour

½ teaspoon baking soda

⅛ teaspoon ground cinnamon

¼ teaspoon kosher salt

1¼ cups thick-cut rolled oats

½ cup pecans, toasted (see Toasting Tips, page 7) and coarsely chopped

½ cup dried apricots (preferably unsulfured), diced into ¼-inch pieces

½ cup (1 stick) unsalted butter, at room temperature

½ cup packed light brown sugar

⅓ cup granulated sugar

1 large egg

½ teaspoon pure vanilla extract

The inspiration for this recipe came from Teri Smith, a dear friend. Oatmeal cookies are her go-to comfort food, and she often bakes them on rainy Seattle days. One thing I love about these cookies is that they're not overly sweet; another is their wonderful chewy texture. The addition of chopped dried apricots (a beautiful and tasty substitute for those ubiquitous raisins) and crisp toasted pecans makes it impossible to eat just one—no matter what the weather.

MAKES TWENTY 3-INCH COOKIES

1. Sift together the flour, baking soda, cinnamon, and salt in a medium bowl. Add the oats, pecans, and apricots and combine thoroughly (I like to use my hands). Set aside.

2. In the bowl of a stand mixer fitted with the paddle attachment or in a large bowl using an electric mixer, mix the butter and sugars on low speed until just combined. Increase the speed to medium and mix for 5 to 8 minutes more, stopping to scrape down the bowl with a rubber spatula as needed. The butter mixture will be light, fluffy, and pale. Add the egg and vanilla and mix on low speed until fully incorporated. Scrape your bowl down, then add the dry ingredients in 3 additions, mixing until just incorporated, about 1 minute. Be careful not to over-mix: the cookies may become tough.

3. Transfer the dough to a large container, cover it, and refrigerate for a minimum of 2 hours. At this point the dough can be formed into cookies or stored in the refrigerator for up to 5 days. This dough also freezes well for up to 3 weeks.

4. Position 2 racks in the center of the oven and preheat to 350°F. Line 2 rimmed baking sheets with parchment paper.

5. Let the cookie dough warm at room temperature for 20 minutes to make portioning easier. Scoop the dough from the bowl with a large spoon or a #30 ice cream scoop and form into 1¾-inch balls. Place about 1½ inches apart on the prepared baking sheets, flattening them to ½ inch thickness while maintaining the circle shape. Bake for 18 to 20 minutes, or until the cookies are golden brown. Halfway through

baking, check the cookies: if they are browning unevenly, rotate the sheets. Cool on the sheet for 10 minutes, then transfer to a wire rack to cool completely. Store in an airtight container at room temperature for up to 4 days.

Nutritious, Delicious Granola Cookies

New to our lineup, these cookies are packed with cranberries, golden raisins, and apricots, along with toasted almonds, pumpkin seeds, and sunflower seeds. They're a veritable powerhouse of nutrition! You may, of course, create your own custom blend of goodies; just be sure to keep the proportion of fruits and nuts about the same. You may also find yourself eating these cookies for breakfast on the run or as an alternative to pricey energy bars with undecipherable ingredients—these are a much better option.

MAKES TWENTY 3½-INCH COOKIES

1. Soak the raisins, cranberries, and apricots in a medium bowl filled with hot water to cover for 20 minutes. Drain and squeeze the fruit gently to remove any excess water; set aside.

2. Sift together the flour, baking soda, baking powder, and salt in another medium bowl. Add the oats, seeds, and almonds and combine thoroughly (I like to use my hands). Set aside.

3. In the bowl of a stand mixer fitted with the paddle attachment or in a large bowl using an electric mixer, cream the butter and sugars. Start on low speed and increase to medium for a total of 5 to 8 minutes, stopping to scrape down the bowl with a rubber spatula as needed. The mixture will be light, fluffy, and pale. Add the egg and vanilla and mix on low speed until fully incorporated, then scrape the bowl down again. Mix in the dry ingredients in 4 additions. After the third addition, add the plumped raisins, cranberries, and apricots along with the final portion of the flour mixture. Mix until the ingredients are just incorporated and the dough is smooth. Be careful not to overmix: the cookies may become tough.

4. Transfer the dough to a large bowl, cover it, and refrigerate for a minimum of 2 hours. At this point the dough can be formed into cookies or stored in the refrigerator for up to 5 days. This dough also freezes well for up to 3 weeks.

5. Position 2 racks in the center of the oven and preheat to 325°F. Line 2 rimmed baking sheets with parchment paper.

6. Let the cookie dough warm at room temperature for 20 minutes to make portioning easier. Scoop the dough from the bowl with a large

¼ cup golden raisins

¼ cup dried cranberries

8 whole dried apricots (preferably unsulfured), cut into ¼-inch dice

1 cup plus 2 tablespoons unbleached all-purpose flour

½ teaspoon baking soda

½ teaspoon baking powder

½ teaspoon kosher salt

¾ cup thick-cut rolled oats

1 tablespoon flax seeds

⅓ cup raw sunflower seeds, toasted (see Toasting Tips, page 7)

¼ cup raw pumpkin seeds, toasted

¼ cup raw almonds (skins on), toasted and coarsely chopped

½ cup (1 stick) unsalted butter

⅓ cup plus 2 tablespoons granulated sugar

⅓ cup plus 2 tablespoons packed light brown sugar

1 large egg

1 teaspoon pure vanilla extract

spoon or a #30 ice cream scoop and form into 1¾-inch balls. Place about 3 inches apart on the prepared baking sheets, flattening them to ½ inch thickness while maintaining the circle shape. Bake for 18 to 20 minutes, or until the cookies are golden brown. After 10 minutes, check the cookies: if they are browning unevenly, rotate the sheets. Repeat with the rest of the dough, allowing the baking sheets to cool between batches. Cool on the sheet for 10 minutes, then transfer to a wire rack to cool completely. Store baked cookies in an airtight container at room temperature for up to 1 week.

Oatmeal Peanut Butter Chocolate Chip Cookies

This one goes out to all you crispy cookie fans. It's a delicious combination of rich, chunky peanut butter, thick rolled oats, caramel-like brown sugar and nuggets of semisweet chocolate. For best results, plan to let the dough rest in the fridge for about 2 hours before baking: you'll get a more tender cookie. This dough holds so well—up to a week—that you can have fresh-baked cookies today and then, at a moment's notice, bake a few more without having to start from scratch. That makes it a hit in my book.

MAKES TWENTY 3½-INCH COOKIES

1. Sift together the flour, baking soda, cinnamon, and salt in a medium bowl. Add the oats and chocolate chips and mix well to combine. Set aside.

2. In the bowl of a stand mixer fitted with the paddle attachment or in a large bowl using an electric mixer, mix the peanut butter, butter, and sugars on low speed until the ingredients are mostly incorporated. Increase the speed to medium and mix for 5 to 8 minutes more, stopping to scrape the bowl with a rubber spatula as needed. The butter mixture will be light, fluffy, and pale. Add the egg and vanilla; mix on low speed until fully incorporated, then scrape the bowl down again. Add the dry ingredients in 3 additions, mixing until just incorporated, about 1 minute. Be careful not to overmix: the cookies may become tough.

3. Transfer the dough to a large bowl, cover it, and refrigerate for a minimum of 2 hours. At this point the dough can be formed into cookies or stored in the refrigerator for up to 7 days. This dough also freezes well for up to 3 weeks.

4. Position 2 racks in the center of the oven and preheat to 325°F. Line 2 rimmed baking sheets with parchment paper.

5. Let the cookie dough warm at room temperature for 20 minutes to make portioning easier. Scoop the dough from the bowl with a large spoon or a #30 ice cream scoop and form into 1¾-inch balls. Place about 2 inches apart on the prepared baking sheets, flattening them to ½ inch thickness while maintaining the circle shape. Bake for 18 to 20 minutes,

1½ cups unbleached all-purpose flour

1½ teaspoons baking soda

¼ teaspoon ground cinnamon

½ teaspoon kosher salt

1½ cups thick-cut rolled oats

¾ cup semisweet chocolate chips, or 3½ ounces semisweet chocolate, chopped into ½-inch pieces

⅔ cup chunky natural peanut butter

14 tablespoons (1¾ sticks) unsalted butter

1 cup packed light brown sugar

1 cup granulated sugar

1 large egg

1½ teaspoons pure vanilla extract

or until the cookies are golden brown. Halfway through baking, check the cookies: if they are browning unevenly, rotate the sheets. Cool on the sheet for 10 minutes, then transfer to a wire rack to cool completely. Store in an airtight container at room temperature for up to 3 days.

Vegan Chocolate Chip Cookies

Chocolate chip is by far our best-selling cookie. This vegan version, with its chewy texture and rich flavor, more than holds its own alongside the much-loved Toll House variety. You'll need a few special ingredients for this recipe. Egg replacement powders are designed to simulate the binding and leavening properties of eggs. Vegan butter is a vegetable-based fat that typically includes a blend of oils (such as soy, palm, and canola), salt, and lecithin. Palm shortening contains no trans fats; it has a semisolid texture and neutral flavor very similar to that of standard vegetable shortening. Finally, be sure to use beet sugar or another sugar that is vegan. All of these are available at your local co-op or specialty market (such as Whole Foods).

MAKES TWENTY 3-INCH COOKIES

1. Sift together the flour, baking soda, egg replacement, and salt in a medium bowl. Add the chocolate chips and mix well to combine. Set aside.

2. In the bowl of a stand mixer fitted with the paddle attachment or in a large bowl using an electric mixer, cream the butter, shortening, sugar, and vanilla. Start on low speed and increase to medium for a total of 5 to 8 minutes, stopping to scrape down the bowl with a rubber spatula as needed. The mixture will be fluffy and very pale. Add the dry ingredients in 3 additions, alternating with the water. Stop halfway and scrape the bowl with a rubber spatula. Mix until just incorporated, about 1 minute. Be careful not to overmix: the cookies may become tough.

3. Transfer the dough to a medium bowl, cover it with plastic wrap, and refrigerate for a minimum of 2 hours. At this point the dough can be formed into cookies or stored in the refrigerator for up to 5 days. This dough also freezes well for up to 3 weeks.

4. Position 2 racks in the center of the oven and preheat to 350°F. Line 2 rimmed baking sheets with parchment paper.

5. Let the cookie dough warm at room temperature for 20 minutes to make portioning easier. Scoop the dough from the bowl with a large spoon or a #30 ice cream scoop and form into 1¾-inch balls.

3 cups unbleached all-purpose flour

1 teaspoon baking soda

2 teaspoons egg replacement powder (see page xxv)

1 teaspoon kosher salt

2½ cups bittersweet chocolate chips

½ cup (1 stick) vegan butter (preferably Earth Balance Vegan Buttery Sticks), at room temperature

⅓ cup palm shortening, at room temperature

¾ cup light brown vegan sugar

1 teaspoon pure vanilla extract

¾ cup water

Place about 2 inches apart on the prepared baking sheets, flattening them to ½ inch thickness while maintaining the circle shape. Bake for 18 to 20 minutes, or until the cookies are golden brown. (These cookies don't spread much, so they'll look a little different than standard chocolate chip cookies.) Cool them on a wire rack for 20 minutes before serving. Store baked cookies in an airtight container at room temperature for up to 3 days.

Car-co-doodles

Not long ago, my daughter and I spent some time researching dog breeds. We were trying to find a new pet—a hybrid that combined several wonderful, irresistible traits. I decided to follow that lead and do some cookie crossbreeding for this recipe. I started with the humble snickerdoodle, but I was looking for a more assertive caramel flavor and wanted to bring in just a hint of bittersweet chocolate. The result is a combination of favorite old-fashioned cookie flavors brings out the best of all three that I call the Car-co-doodle.

MAKES SIXTEEN 3½-INCH COOKIES

1. Sift together the flour, cream of tartar, baking soda, and salt in a medium bowl. Add the chocolate pieces and set aside.

2. In the bowl of a stand mixer fitted with the paddle attachment or in a large bowl using an electric mixer, cream the butter and brown sugar. Start on low speed and increase to medium for a total of 5 to 8 minutes, stopping to scrape down the bowl with a rubber spatula as needed. The mixture will be light, fluffy, and pale. Add the vanilla and then the egg, mixing on low speed until fully incorporated, then scrape the bowl down again. Gradually add the dry ingredients, mixing until they're just incorporated and the dough is smooth, about 30 seconds. Be careful not to overmix: the cookies may become tough.

3. Transfer the dough to a medium bowl, cover it, and refrigerate for a minimum of 2 hours. At this point the dough can be formed into cookies or stored in the refrigerator for up to 5 days. This dough also freezes well for up to 3 weeks.

4. Position 2 racks in the center of the oven and preheat to 325°F. Line 2 rimmed baking sheets with parchment paper.

5. Make the garnishing sugar: stir the granulated sugar and cinnamon together in a small bowl.

6. Let the cookie dough warm at room temperature for 20 minutes to make portioning easier. Scoop the dough from the bowl with a large spoon or a #30 ice cream scoop and form into 1¾-inch balls. Dip the balls of dough into the garnishing sugar and then place about 2 inches apart on the prepared baking sheets. Slightly flatten the cookies,

1⅓ cups unbleached all-purpose flour

1 teaspoon cream of tartar

½ teaspoon baking soda

¼ teaspoon kosher salt

3 ounces bittersweet chocolate, chopped into ½-inch pieces

½ cup (1 stick) unsalted butter, at room temperature

1 cup packed light brown sugar

1 teaspoon pure vanilla extract

1 large egg

½ cup granulated sugar

2 teaspoons ground cinnamon

retaining the circle shape. Bake just until the cookies are set, 15 to 18 minutes. Halfway through baking, check the cookies: if they are browning unevenly, rotate the sheets. The cookies will be a very light golden brown (don't let them get any darker—underbaking the cookies slightly helps preserve their distinctive chewy texture). Cool on the sheets for 10 minutes, then transfer to a wire rack to cool completely. Store baked cookies in an airtight container at room temperature for up to 4 days.

Gluten-Free Chocolate-Chocolate Melts

These cookies rank as the all-time favorite among my gluten-free friends. They're sweet and very chocolaty and bake flat with multiple textures: a crackled top, crispy edges, and a soft center. They make for a decadent ice cream sandwich—close your eyes and envision a filling of almond sorbet and fresh raspberries . . .

MAKES TWO DOZEN 2-INCH COOKIES

3 tablespoons brown rice flour

2 tablespoons potato starch flour

2 tablespoons tapioca flour

¼ teaspoon kosher salt

⅓ cup bittersweet chocolate chips

¼ cup (½ stick) unsalted butter

⅓ cup semisweet chocolate chips

¾ cup sugar

2 large eggs

½ teaspoon pure vanilla extract

1. Position 2 racks in the center of the oven and preheat to 350°F. Line 2 rimmed baking sheets with parchment paper and set aside.

2. Sift together the flours and salt in a small bowl. Add the bittersweet chocolate chips and mix well to combine. Set aside.

3. Melt the butter and semisweet chocolate chips over medium heat in a double boiler or a stainless steel bowl set over a small saucepan filled with about 2 inches of water. (The bowl should not touch the water.) Whisk together the chocolate and butter to combine. When the mixture has completely melted, remove the bowl and set aside to cool for 5 minutes.

4. Add the sugar to the cooled chocolate mixture and whisk until it has come together into a paste; it will remain a bit grainy. Add the eggs one at a time, fully incorporating the first before adding the second. Stir in the vanilla. Add the dry ingredients in 3 additions, whisking each addition until incorporated. This will take about 1 minute.

5. The dough will be very liquidy. Scoop it from the bowl with a tablespoon or #30 ice cream scoop and place about 2 inches apart on the prepared baking sheets. Each pool of dough should be about 1¼ inches in diameter; the baked cookies will expand to about 2 inches. Bake for 10 to 12 minutes, or until the tops are crackled and the edges look dry; the center will look slightly wet or underbaked. (This cookie will continue to bake and set up as it cools.) Halfway through baking, check the cookies: if they are browning unevenly, rotate the sheets. Cool on the sheet for 20 minutes, then transfer to a wire rack to cool completely. Repeat with the rest of the dough, allowing the baking sheets to cool between batches. Store these fragile cookies for up to 4 days in a shallow, airtight plastic container at room temperature, layered between sheets of parchment paper.

Pistachio Shortbread Cookies

At Macrina, we include these buttery-rich shortbread cookies in our Christmas Cookie Box each year. This easy recipe comes in handy during the busy holiday season—simply roll the dough into a log, slice, and bake as needed! The natural pale green color of the pistachios in the cookie points to holiday celebrations, but the flavors—subtle yet distinctive—will call you to make the recipe throughout the year.

MAKES TWENTY 2-INCH COOKIES

1 cup unbleached all-purpose flour

¼ cup sugar

½ teaspoon kosher salt

½ cup raw pistachios

½ teaspoon pure vanilla extract

½ cup (1 stick) chilled unsalted butter, cut into ¼-inch pieces

¼ cup sugar, for garnish

1. Pulse the flour, sugar, salt, pistachios, and vanilla in the bowl of a food processor for 1 to 2 minutes until the pistachios are finely ground. Scatter the butter pieces in the food processor and pulse several times to cut the butter into the flour. At first the mixture will have a coarse, crumbly texture; then it will become a paste. Watch it carefully: food processors work very fast and can easily overmix the dough. Stop pulsing when it just comes together.

2. Turn the dough out onto a lightly floured work surface and form into a log about 2 inches in diameter and 10 inches long. (If the dough is too sticky, chilling it for 10 minutes will make it easier to work with. A bit of water on your hands also helps.) Place the log on a piece of plastic wrap or parchment paper. Tightly roll the wrap around the log and twist the ends to seal them securely. Refrigerate for at least 2 hours or overnight. At this point the dough can be cut into cookies or stored in the refrigerator for up to 5 days. This dough also freezes well if wrapped tightly in plastic for up to 3 weeks.

3. Position 2 racks in the center of the oven and preheat to 325°F. Line 2 rimmed baking sheets with parchment paper and set aside.

4. Cut the chilled cookie dough into ½-inch-thick coins and place about 2 inches apart on the prepared baking sheets. Lightly brush the top of each cookie with water and sprinkle with sugar. Bake for 15 to 18 minutes, or until the cookies are golden brown on the top and bottom. Cool on the sheet for 5 minutes, then transfer to a wire rack to cool completely. Store baked cookies in an airtight container at room temperature for up to 2 weeks. For gift giving, stack the cookies, slip them into a clear cellophane bag, and tie with a ribbon.

*Overlake Hospital: A New Partnership *for* Good Health *

I've been involved in the wholesale artisan bread business for more than twenty years. Our customers are respected local restaurants, quaint coffeehouses offering baked goods and sandwiches, and specialty markets that support other artisan businesses and the farm-to-table movement. You can only imagine my deep happiness when Macrina sales manager extraordinaire Rebecca Early told me of a new customer in a completely new category: Overlake Hospital, an award-winning hospital complex in nearby Bellevue, Washington.

We all know that hospital food has a poor reputation. How can it be that medical establishments are still, for the most part, serving nutrient-poor processed foods, trans-fat-laden baked goods, and canned vegetables to their staff and patients? It's counterintuitive—people are there to heal, and food plays a large role in that process.

On that front, Overlake is a leader in the Pacific Northwest, acting not only to upgrade its food quality, but to support our local economy at the same time. The hospital has made the connection between the foods people eat—good and bad—and their overall health. Its food service department operates three cafés and two espresso kiosks, but most importantly, it provides 18,000 patient meals a month. Overlake was the first area hospital to purchase local cage-free eggs, which it uses exclusively. Vegetables, mostly organic, are sourced through a local produce company that buys directly from local farmers. And the fresh meat it prepares is raised nearby, in Washington state or Northern California.

Bread is where we come in. Macrina Bakery provides the hospital with most of its bread and baked goods: brioche for French toast, sliced artisan breads and rolls for a variety of beautiful fresh sandwiches, and other items for patients' meals. Our fresh-baked cookies grace the baskets prominently displayed in all the cafés, and our scones and muffins greet the staff as they begin their day. The response from café customers, medical staff, and patients alike has been overwhelmingly positive—they can't help but get an emotional lift when they're able to choose high-quality, fresh foods.

Providing good food at an institution whose purpose is to heal your ailments only makes sense to me. Overlake is setting an example for other institutions to make changes where they can—real changes that impact people's health, and perhaps inspire them to take their own small steps to make the world a better place. Of all the esteemed customers Macrina has the privilege to work with, I am so very proud that we're partners with this respected hospital.

Chocolate Hazelnut Shortbread Cookies

Kilian Weigand was the first pastry chef I worked with, at the elegant Bostonian Hotel back in 1985, and I'm so grateful I had that opportunity. He's a character and a true perfectionist. This recipe comes from his repertoire; over the years I've tweaked it with additions of dried fruit, chocolate, or spices according to my whim of the moment. Delicious by itself, this cookie is also scrumptious served with poached peaches and lightly sweetened whipped cream. Simply warm the cookies in a 325°F oven for 5 minutes, then sandwich the fruit between them and place a big dollop of whipped cream on the side.

MAKES ONE DOZEN 3-INCH SQUARE COOKIES

1¼ cups cake flour

¼ teaspoon kosher salt

⅓ cup good-quality chocolate chips, or 2 ounces bittersweet chocolate, coarsely chopped

¾ cup blanched hazelnuts, toasted (see Toasting Tips, page 7)

10 tablespoons (1¼ sticks) unsalted butter, at room temperature

½ cup sugar

1 large egg

1. Sift the flour and salt together in a medium bowl. Add the chocolate chips and hazelnuts and transfer to the bowl of the food processer. Pulse for 1 minute, or until the hazelnuts are finely ground. The chocolate will still be a little chunky. Pour into a medium bowl and set aside.

2. In the bowl of a stand mixer fitted with the paddle attachment or in a large bowl using an electric mixer, cream the butter and sugar. Start on low speed and increase to medium for a total of 5 to 8 minutes, stopping to scrape down the bowl with a rubber spatula as needed. The mixture will be light, fluffy, and pale. Add the egg and mix on low speed until fully incorporated, then scrape the bowl down again. Gradually add the dry ingredients, mixing until the ingredients are just incorporated and the dough is smooth, about 30 seconds. Be careful not to overmix: the cookies may become tough.

3. Turn the dough out onto a lightly floured work surface and form it into a 7-by-7-inch square. Wrap it tightly in plastic wrap and refrigerate for a minimum of 2 hours. At this point the dough can be formed into cookies or stored in the refrigerator for up to 4 days. This dough also freezes well for up to 3 weeks.

4. Position 2 racks in the center of the oven and preheat to 325°F. Line 2 rimmed baking sheets with parchment paper.

5. Generously flour your work surface and cut the chilled dough in half. You will need to let it warm a bit to make it easier to work with. Gently knead one portion of the dough, folding it onto itself several times; it should become very malleable. Using a rolling pin, roll it out into a 6-by-9-inch rectangle about ¼ inch thick. (This dough is made

with lots of butter, so it will tend to stick—add more flour to your work surface as needed. If the dough becomes too soft to work with, refrigerate for about 10 minutes to firm it up, then continue rolling.) Repeat with the other dough half.

6. Cut each piece of dough into six 3-by-3-inch cookies. Using an offset spatula, transfer the cookies onto the prepared baking sheets, placing them 2 inches apart. Use the tines of a fork to create a decorative design—I like to press on each of the four corners, creating diagonal lines. Chill the sheets in the freezer for 10 minutes, then bake the cookies for 18 to 20 minutes, or until the tops look slightly dry and the edges are golden brown. Halfway through baking, check the cookies: if they are browning unevenly, rotate the sheets. Cool the cookies on the sheets for 10 minutes, then transfer to a wire rack to cool completely. Store in an airtight container at room temperature for up to 1 week.

Semolina Sesame Cookies

These cookies are inspired by acclaimed baker Carol Field, who gathered a collection of wonderful regional recipes from bakers, grandmothers, and chefs on her travels through Italy. The essence of this recipe came from one of her books (I have them all!), and is so typically Italian. The semolina, a coarsely ground wheat flour used widely for making pasta, lends a beautiful crisp texture, and the sesame seeds make them a classic accompaniment to a sweetened shot of espresso. Buttery and not too sweet, they'll totally satisfy that 4 p.m. nosh need!

MAKES EIGHTEEN 3-INCH COOKIES

¾ cup plus 2 tablespoons unbleached all-purpose flour

⅓ cup plus 1 tablespoon semolina flour

¼ teaspoon kosher salt

7 tablespoons unsalted butter, at room temperature

⅓ cup plus 1 tablespoon sugar

1 large egg

¼ cup sesame seeds

1. Position 2 racks in the center of the oven and preheat to 325°F. Line 2 rimmed baking sheets with parchment paper. Set aside.

2. Sift together the flours and salt in a medium bowl.

3. In the bowl of a stand mixer fitted with the paddle attachment or in a large bowl using an electric mixer, cream the butter and sugar. Start on low speed and increase to medium for a total of 5 to 8 minutes, stopping to scrape down the bowl with a rubber spatula as needed. The mixture will be light, fluffy, and pale. Add the egg and mix on low speed until fully incorporated, then scrape the bowl down again. Gradually add the dry ingredients, mixing until they're just incorporated and the dough is smooth, about 1 minute. Be careful not to overmix: the cookies may become tough.

4. Turn the dough out onto a lightly floured work surface. Divide it into 4 equal pieces, then roll each piece into a ½-inch-wide rope. Use a ruler to measure and then cut the ropes into 5-inch segments. Each segment will become a cookie. If the dough is too soft, chill for 10 minutes to make it easier to handle.

5. Lay each rope in an S shape, 1 inch apart, on the prepared baking sheets. Tuck the ends under and compress slightly. Chill the sheets in the freezer for 20 minutes to help the cookies hold their shape while baking. (You may also freeze the cookies at this point, covered tightly, for up to 1 week. Let them thaw for about 20 minutes before baking.)

6. Brush each cookie with a little bit of water and top with the sesame seeds. Bake for 18 to 20 minutes, or until the cookies are light golden brown. Cool on the sheet for 5 minutes, then transfer to a wire rack to cool completely. Stored in an airtight container at room temperature, these cookies keep their great flavor for at least 1 week.

Pecan Wafers

1 cup unbleached all-purpose flour

2 tablespoons plus 1 teaspoon whole wheat flour

½ cup cornstarch

1 teaspoon baking soda

¼ teaspoon kosher salt

½ cup (1 stick) unsalted butter, at room temperature

3 tablespoons sugar

2 tablespoons dark molasses (preferably blackstrap)

½ cup pecan pieces, toasted (see Toasting Tips, page 7)

¼ cup sugar, for garnish

Similar to an English digestive biscuit, these wafers swing both sweet and savory. I'm willing to bet that this is a cookie unlike any other in your repertoire: crisp, thin, with slight overtones of molasses and roasted pecans, all topped with a light shimmer of sugar. Pair these delicious wafers with a favorite artisan cheese or serve them alongside vanilla bean ice cream with warmed plums and port for dessert. Or just eat them as a snack. Caution: they're addictive!

MAKES THIRTY-TWO 2-INCH COOKIES

1. Sift together the flours, cornstarch, baking soda, and salt in a medium-size bowl. Set aside.

2. In the bowl of a stand mixer fitted with the paddle attachment or in a large bowl using an electric mixer, cream the butter and sugar. Start mixing on low speed and increase to medium speed, for a total of 3 minutes. Add the molasses and continue creaming on medium speed for another 4 minutes, or until the mixture is light, fluffy, and light caramel-brown colored. Scrape down the bowl with a rubber spatula to ensure all the ingredients are well incorporated.

3. Pulse the pecans and 1 cup of the dry ingredients in the bowl of a food processor until the pecans are finely ground, about 1 minute. Add this back to the dry ingredients and mix well.

4. With the mixer on low speed, gradually add the dry ingredients, mixing until they're just incorporated and the dough is smooth, about 1 minute. Be careful not to overmix: the cookies may become tough. If the dry ingredients aren't fully incorporated, mix them in with the spatula.

5. Turn the dough out onto a lightly floured work surface and form into a log 2 inches in diameter and about 8 inches long. (If the dough is too sticky, chilling it for 10 minutes will make it easier to work with. A bit of water on your hands also helps.) Place the log on a piece of plastic wrap or parchment paper. Tightly roll the wrap around the log and twist the ends to seal them securely. Refrigerate for at least 2 hours. At this point the dough can be cut into cookies or stored, well wrapped, in the refrigerator for up to 5 days. This dough also freezes well for up to 3 weeks.

6. Position two racks in the center of the oven and preheat to 325°F. Line 2 rimmed baking sheets with parchment paper.

7. Cut the chilled cookie dough into ¼-inch-thick coins and place 1 inch apart on the prepared baking sheets. Lightly brush the top of each cookie with a little water and sprinkle lightly with the sugar. Bake for 15 to 18 minutes, or until the cookies are dark golden brown on top. Cool on the sheet for 5 minutes, then transfer to a wire rack to cool completely. Stored in an airtight container at room temperature, these cookies will stay fresh for up to 2 weeks.

PIES

MAKING PIES, all day long—I never tire of it. There's something about pies that has always intrigued me. Similar to breads, they require only a few ingredients—but how you put them together makes all the difference between a remarkable pie and an average one. I made my first pie when I was twelve years old, from cherries picked in our backyard. I was so proud of my bountiful bowl. After laboriously pitting each one and then tossing them with sugar and flour, I loaded the cherries into a pie shell my mother had readied for me. We baked it with watchful eyes and made it the centerpiece after dinner. To my great surprise, I had not used nearly enough sugar or flour. We were left with a savory cherry soup!

Practice does pay off, and I've been working at perfecting pies ever since. In this pursuit, I've learned to be particular about a few details. Choosing ripe seasonal fruit, taking care to cut the fruit to an appropriate size, and draining off any excess juices are important steps. The other half of the equation is the dough. Sticking to just a few basic rules is key: keep all the ingredients as cold as possible (especially the fats); handle the dough lightly, taking care not to overwork it; and roll it to a thickness that will support the pie but not compete with the fruit by being too heavy or bulky at the edges.

This collection of recipes starts with our master recipe for Flaky Pie Dough: it's so tasty and versatile that I decided to feature it in many of the recipes in this chapter. I made a commitment to modernize it a few years back; the main change was to eliminate the solid vegetable shortening in favor of palm shortening, which has no trans fats. Give it a try and behold the flaky—and healthy—results!

Read on, discovering imaginative ways to work with raspberries, rhubarb, cherries, apples, peaches, coconut, and bananas. There are traditional double-crusted pies and open-faced galettes, individual treats such as tartlets and hand pies, and a winning fruit crisp recipe for impromptu parties.

Over the years I've gathered a repertoire of favorite fruit combinations, experimented with different levels of sweetness, and tested many a pie crust recipe. This chapter is filled with these results and includes many of our customers' favorite recipes. At whatever age you started baking, let these recipes inspire you to celebrate the seasons with fresh-baked pies!

Master Recipe: Flaky Pie Dough

2½ cups plus 2 tablespoons unbleached all-purpose flour

1½ teaspoons kosher salt

14 tablespoons (1¾ sticks) chilled unsalted butter, cut into ¼-inch pieces

½ cup chilled palm or other no-trans-fat shortening, cut into pea-size pieces

½ cup ice water

This is Macrina's most versatile pastry dough. We bake it into fluted tart rings for tangy lemon tarts and form it into ruffled, free-form galettes, both sweet and savory. This recipe was updated a few years ago, and solid vegetable shortening was replaced with palm shortening, which has no trans fats. Then we recalibrated the ratio of shortening to butter and came up with this flaky, delicious pie dough. The healthier shortening is quite soft at room temperature, so be sure to keep the dough well chilled for the best results. If you have scraps or leftover pie dough from the first day, wrap well in plastic and store in the refrigerator for up to 3 days. Freezing is also is an option: the dough will keep, well wrapped, for up to 1 month. That being said, I rarely wrap up scraps—instead, I like to brush them with melted butter, sprinkle with cinnamon-sugar, twist, and then bake at 350°F for 10 minutes, or until the pieces are golden brown . . . that's what my mom used to do!

MAKES ENOUGH FOR ONE 9-INCH DOUBLE-CRUSTED PIE, ONE 10-INCH RUSTIC GALETTE, OR MULTIPLE SMALL PIES OR TARTLETS

1. In the bowl of a stand mixer fitted with the paddle attachment, combine the flour and salt. Add half of the butter pieces and turn the mixer quickly on and off a few times using a low speed. (This is a way of gradually cutting the butter into the flour without sending the flour skyward.) Add the remaining butter and continue mixing on low speed until the mixture is coarse and crumbly, about 2 minutes. Add the shortening pieces to the dough. Continue mixing on low speed until it is crumbly again, about 1 minute. Add the ice water all at once and mix on low speed for about 30 seconds, just until it is incorporated. The dough will now look almost like cookie dough, with no dry parts at the bottom of the bowl. (If you are making the dough by hand, follow the same procedure, using a pastry cutter to incorporate the butter and shortening, and a rubber spatula to mix in the water. Mix just until all the dry ingredients are incorporated.)

2. Next, you'll shape the dough into flat disks or squares, then wrap and chill them in the refrigerator. (Preshaping the dough greatly helps once it comes time to roll it out; the dough will soften evenly and roll easily to the finished dimensions. Resting the dough in the refrigerator re-chills the fats, contributing to the crust's overall flakiness, and allows the glutens to relax, which also makes rolling much easier.)

3. Dust your hands with flour and transfer the dough from the bowl onto a lightly floured work surface (chilled marble is ideal). Depending on which recipe you're making, choose one of the following options, taking care not to overwork the dough; the shapes don't need to be perfect.

To make a standard double-crust pie: Divide the dough into 2 rough balls: one should be about two-thirds of the dough and the other about a third. Pat each ball of dough into a disk about ¾ inch thick. Wrap each disk tightly in plastic wrap and refrigerate until thoroughly chilled, about 1 hour.

To make a lattice-top pie: Divide the dough into 2 rough balls: one should be about two-thirds of the dough and the other about one-third. Pat the larger ball of dough into a disk about ¾ inch thick. Pat the smaller piece into a rough square of the same thickness. Wrap each piece tightly in plastic wrap and refrigerate until thoroughly chilled, about 1 hour.

To make a galette: Pat the dough into a large disk about 1 inch thick. Wrap tightly in plastic wrap and refrigerate until thoroughly chilled, about 1 hour.

To make hand pies or tartlets: Divide the dough into 2 rough balls and pat each into equal-size disks about ¾ inch thick. Wrap each disk tightly in plastic wrap and refrigerate until thoroughly chilled, about 1 hour.

4. Now you're ready to bake any of the pies or pastries that follow.

Apple–Brown Sugar Pie

8 medium Granny Smith apples (about 2½ pounds), peeled, cored, and sliced into ½-inch wedges

1 cup plus 2 tablespoons granulated sugar, divided

¼ cup plus 1 heaping tablespoon unbleached all-purpose flour, divided

½ cup (1 stick) unsalted butter, at room temperature

½ cup packed light brown sugar

1 teaspoon ground cinnamon

1 recipe Flaky Pie Dough for a double-crust pie (page 124)

1 large egg beaten with 1 tablespoon water, for egg wash

Lightly sweetened crème fraîche or whipped cream, for serving

At Macrina, we take apple pies seriously! And between using our classic Flaky Pie Dough and taking just one easy extra step, this may be one of the best you've ever made. It's packed with lots of tart-sweet Granny Smith apples that are briefly prebaked; this helps concentrate their flavors and, importantly, cooks off the excess juices that would otherwise make the bottom crust soggy. The addition of brown sugar butter melting over the apples adds a luscious, caramel-tinged lacing of sweetness.

MAKES ONE 9-INCH PIE

1. Line 2 rimmed baking sheets with parchment paper.

2. Put the apples in a large bowl. In a small bowl, mix 1 cup of the granulated sugar and ¼ cup of the flour. Pour over the apples and toss thoroughly—the wedges should be completely coated. Spread the apples evenly over the prepared baking sheets and bake for 15 to 20 minutes, or until the apples are just tender. Halfway through baking, redistribute the apples to encourage even baking. Cool them on the baking sheets for about 5 minutes. Carefully pour the excess juices into a bowl and reserve. Cool the apples completely at room temperature or refrigerate to speed up the process.

3. Using a fork, mash the butter, brown sugar, cinnamon, and the remaining heaping tablespoon flour in a medium bowl until well mixed. Dot this brown sugar butter randomly onto the apples and toss thoroughly. (You don't want to have concentrations of the butter—it should be dotted throughout the apples.)

4. Remove the dough from the refrigerator and let stand at room temperature for 10 minutes to soften slightly. On a floured work surface, roll the larger disk out into a circle roughly 15 inches in diameter and ⅛ inch thick; this is your bottom crust. (Check frequently to make sure the dough isn't sticking; add flour as needed to the dough and work surface.) Fold the dough in half and transfer it to a 9-inch pie pan. Place the dough in one half of the pan, then unfold, draping it evenly over the entire pan. (This is the easiest way to move the dough without breaking it.) Gently fit the dough into the pan, then trim excess (clean scissors work well for this), leaving a 1-inch overhang.

5. Roll the smaller disk out into a circle roughly 10 inches in diameter and ⅛ inch thick. Invert another 9-inch pie pan on top of the dough and use a small, sharp knife to cut a circle slightly larger than the pan. This is your top crust. Cut six 2-inch slots (or any pattern of your choice) in the middle to vent steam from the pie as it bakes. Using a pastry brush, paint egg wash around the outer ½ inch of the bottom crust.

6. Spoon the filling into the shell, lightly packing the apples and leveling the top. Invert the top crust over the filling, and press down lightly on the egg-washed edge. If the dough extends farther than the pan, cut away the excess. (Bulky pie edges can break during the baking process or remain underbaked when the rest of the pie is finished.)

7. Brush the top crust with the egg wash. Fold the bottom crust overhang up over about ½ inch of the top crust, pressing the layers of dough together. With a fork or your fingers, crimp the edge decoratively, then brush with a little more egg wash. Sprinkle the remaining 2 tablespoons granulated sugar evenly over the top of the pie.

8. Position a rack in the center of the oven and preheat to 350°F.

9. Chill the pie in the freezer for 30 minutes. (Don't be tempted to skip this step! The freezer will firm up the pie dough—which by this time will have become fairly soft from handling. Rechilling the butter will prevent the crust from shrinking, make the dough less apt to fall, and create a flakier finished product.)

10. Increase oven temperature to 375°F. Place the pie on a rimmed baking sheet and bake for 30 minutes. Reduce oven temperature to 350°F and bake until the top is deep brown and the filling is bubbling, about 1 hour. Cool the pie for about 1 hour before serving to let it set up.

11. To serve, spoon some of the reserved apple juice to pool on each plate, and top with a slice of pie and a dollop of lightly sweetened crème fraîche or whipped cream.

Raspberry Rhubarb Lattice-Top Pie

Lattice-top pies are the prettiest of all. Do try your hand at making the alternating strips, creating a beautiful lacelike pie top. (If you're ambitious, you can weave the strips—but I think it's just as effective to simply lay them atop one another). The deep red color of the fruit peeking from the lattice is just spectacular. The raspberries and rhubarb are lightly sweetened and seasoned with a hint of cinnamon, fresh orange zest, and almond extract. If, come springtime, you have your eyes on fresh rhubarb and can't wait for local raspberries, individually frozen, unsweetened raspberries are a great substitute.

MAKES ONE 9-INCH PIE

1. Combine ½ cup of the granulated sugar, cornstarch, cinnamon, cloves, and orange zest in a medium bowl. Mix well and add the rhubarb, tossing to coat all the pieces. Transfer the rhubarb to a large sauté pan over medium low heat. Toss the rhubarb frequently for 3 to 5 minutes; the fruit will just begin to soften, and a bit of slightly thickened sauce will form. Pour into medium bowl and cool for 30 minutes.

2. Combine the remaining ¼ cup granulated sugar and the vanilla and almond extracts in a separate medium bowl. Mix well and add the raspberries, tossing gently to coat. Add the raspberries to the cooled rhubarb and gently toss to combine well. Cover and refrigerate filling until needed.

3. Remove the dough from the refrigerator and let stand at room temperature for 10 minutes to soften slightly. On a floured work surface, roll the larger disk out into a circle roughly 15 inches in diameter and ⅛ inch thick; this is your bottom crust. (Check frequently to make sure the dough isn't sticking; add flour as needed to the dough and work surface.) Fold the dough in half and transfer it to a 9-inch pie pan. Place the dough in one half of the pan, then unfold, draping it evenly over the entire pan. (This is the easiest way to move the dough without breaking it.) Gently pat the dough into the pan, then trim excess (clean scissors work well for this), leaving a 1-inch overhang. Using a pastry brush, paint egg wash around the outside edge of the bottom crust.

4. Roll the smaller disk out into a 10-inch square about ⅛ inch thick. Using a fluted pastry wheel (a wheeled pastry cutter similar to a pizza cutter) or a sharp knife, cut the square into ¾-inch-wide strips. (You can either eyeball this or use a straightedge to guide your cuts.) If the

Ingredients

¾ cup granulated sugar, divided

2 tablespoons cornstarch

1 teaspoon ground cinnamon

½ teaspoon ground cloves

1 teaspoon orange zest

6 stalks fresh rhubarb (about 1 pound, 6 ounces), trimmed and cut into 1-inch pieces

2 tablespoons pure vanilla extract

1 teaspoon pure almond extract

3 cups (about 2 pints) fresh raspberries, plus a few for garnish

1 recipe Flaky Pie Dough for a lattice-top pie (page 124)

1 large egg beaten with 1 tablespoon water, for egg wash

¼ cup turbinado sugar, for garnish

Confectioners' sugar, for serving

dough is warming too quickly, re-cover it and return it to the refrigerator to chill for several minutes.

5. Spoon the filling into the shell, gently leveling the top. Lay a strip horizontally across the top edge of the pie, pressing the ends onto the egg-washed edge and pinching off any excess dough. Brush the strip with egg wash. Next, lay a vertical strip across the left edge of the pie, following the same procedure. Continue laying the strips, alternating horizontal and vertical pieces, until the top is covered. (If you run short of strips, you can piece them together from scraps, gluing them with a little egg wash.) Brush egg wash onto the edge of the pie. Fold the bottom crust up over the edges of the lattice, creating a ½-inch edge, pressing the layers of dough together. With a fork or your fingers, crimp the edge decoratively, then brush the edges once more with egg wash and sprinkle with turbinado sugar.

6. Position a rack in the center of the oven and preheat to 375°F.

7. Chill the pie in the freezer for 30 minutes. (Don't be tempted to skip this step! The freezer will firm up the pie dough—which by this time will have become fairly soft from handling. Rechilling the butter will prevent the crust from shrinking, make the dough less apt to fall, and create a flakier finished product.)

8. Place the pie on a rimmed baking sheet and bake for 20 minutes. Reduce oven temperature to 350°F and bake until the top is golden brown and the filling is bubbling, about another hour and 10 minutes. Cool the pie for about 1 hour before serving to let it set up.

9. To serve, I like to sprinkle a little confectioners' sugar onto the rim of the pie and garnish with a few fresh raspberries.

Peach and Brown Sugar Galette

5 ripe medium peaches

½ cup plus 1 tablespoon granulated sugar, divided

3 tablespoons cornstarch

¼ teaspoon lemon zest

¼ cup (½ stick) unsalted butter, at room temperature

3 tablespoons light brown sugar

½ teaspoon pure vanilla extract

½ teaspoon pure almond extract

¼ teaspoon ground cinnamon

1½ teaspoons unbleached all-purpose flour

1 recipe Flaky Pie Dough for a galette (page 124)

1 large egg beaten with 1 tablespoon water, for egg wash

Sweetened whipped cream or ice cream, for serving

Each year at the height of summer, our local Metropolitan Market stores feature a "Peach-o-Rama," offering the most luscious local peaches they can find. Many come from Pence Orchards in Eastern Washington's Yakima Valley. Pence is a fourth-generation family farm that picks its peaches only when they've reached a minimum level of 13 on the Brix sugar scale—prime peach sweetness! At Macrina, we use those perfect peaches to make this free-form pie. Simply roll the dough out into a large circle, place the fruit in the center, and lift the remaining dough up onto the fruit, making a lovely ruffled galette.

MAKES ONE 9-INCH GALETTE

1. Line a rimmed baking sheet with parchment paper. Put a handful of ice into a medium bowl and fill it three-quarters full with cold water.

2. With a paring knife, cut an X on the bottom of each peach. Fill a medium saucepan with water and bring to it to a boil over high heat. When the water is boiling, gently add the peaches. (This is called blanching, and it will enable you to easily peel the fruit.) When the skin around the cuts starts to curl—about 30 to 60 seconds depending on the ripeness of the fruit—pull the peaches out with a slotted spoon and immediately immerse them in the ice water. (This is called shocking, and it stops the cooking process).

3. When the peaches are cool enough to handle, remove their skins and cut the peaches into ½-inch wedges. In a medium bowl, toss them with ½ cup of the granulated sugar. Let sit for about 20 minutes to allow the sugar to pull out any extra juice. Pour the peaches into a strainer fitted over a bowl. Toss the strained peaches with the cornstarch and lemon zest, and reserve ¼ cup of the juice to add to the galette just before baking.

4. Using a fork, mash the butter, brown sugar, vanilla and almond extracts, cinnamon, and flour in a medium bowl until well mixed. (I call this "fruit pie butter," and it's the secret flavoring that sets many of Macrina's fruit pies apart from others'!)

5. Remove the dough from the refrigerator and let stand at room temperature for 10 minutes to soften slightly. On a floured work surface, roll it out into a circle roughly 15 inches in diameter and ⅛ inch thick. (Check frequently to make sure the dough isn't sticking; add flour as

needed to the dough and work surface.) Using a knife or plastic pastry scraper, cut away any uneven edges. Fold the dough in half and transfer to the prepared baking sheet. Unfold the dough and center it on the pan.

6. Arrange the peaches in the center, forming a 9-inch circle approximately 1½ inches high and leaving a 3-inch border of dough. Dot the peaches evenly with the pie butter. Lift the dough border up and fold it over the fruit, making gathers or pleats; there will be a 3- to 4-inch circle of fruit left exposed. Pour the reserved peach juice into the center of the galette. Brush the dough evenly and thoroughly with egg wash (any uncovered areas will be apparent after baking).

7. Position a rack in the center of the oven and preheat to 375°F.

8. Chill the galette in the freezer for 30 to 45 minutes. (Don't be tempted to skip this step! The freezer will firm up the pie dough—which by this time will have become fairly soft from handling. Rechilling the butter will prevent the crust from shrinking, make the dough less apt to fall, and create a flakier finished product.)

9. Sprinkle the galette with the remaining 1 tablespoon granulated sugar. Bake for 1 hour, or until the galette is deep golden brown and the juices are bubbling. Cool the galette for about 45 minutes to let it set up; if you slice it right away, all the hot juices will flow out!

10. To serve, cut the slightly warm or room-temperature galette (still on the baking sheet) into wedges. Transfer the pieces to plates and add a dollop of sweetened whipped cream or ice cream. Or you can move the whole galette to a decorative plate: cut the parchment around the base of the galette, slide a removable tart pan bottom under the paper, and gently transfer the galette to the dish, leaving the paper in place (personally, I like its rustic look) or pulling it out.

Nutella Banana Hand Pies

Isn't it funny that foods cycle in popularity much as clothing trends or popular colors do? While pies have always held a spot in my heart, the rest of the country has rediscovered pies and is currently singing their praises. These hand pies (similar to turnovers) are filled with sweetened fresh bananas, brandy, and Nutella—that irresistible blend of chocolate and hazelnut butter. If you've stashed some pie dough in the fridge or freezer, these hand pies make a quick homemade treat to delight your dinner guests. Simply serve warm with a scoop of ice cream—coconut, chocolate, raspberry swirl, or vanilla bean come to mind—and a drizzle of brandy.

MAKES FOUR 6-BY-2-INCH PIES

1. Line a rimmed baking sheet with parchment paper.

2. Remove the dough from the refrigerator and let stand at room temperature for about 10 minutes to soften slightly. On a floured work surface, roll the dough out from the center of the disk until it's about ⅛ inch thick. (Check frequently to make sure the dough isn't sticking; add flour as needed to the dough and work surface.) Using a plate, plastic lid, or other object as a guide, cut out four 6½-inch rounds and transfer them to the prepared baking sheet. Store these in the refrigerator while you prepare the filling.

3. In the bowl of a food processor, pulse the granulated sugar and hazelnuts until the hazelnuts are finely ground. Set aside.

4. Pour the butter over the bananas in a medium bowl. Add the brown sugar and brandy and toss to combine. Add the Nutella and gently mix just until it streaks the bananas. Spoon the filling equally onto the lower half of each dough round, leaving a 1-inch border along the bottom edge. Brush the border with the egg wash and then fold the top half of the circle over the lower half, creating a half-moon shape. Even the edges and gently press with a fork to seal. Cut a ½-inch steam vent on the top of each pie, then brush the pies with egg wash and sprinkle with the hazelnut sugar.

5. Position a rack in the center of the oven and preheat to 375°F.

6. Chill the pies in the freezer for 20 minutes. (Don't be tempted to skip this step! The freezer will firm up the pie dough—which by this

½ recipe Flaky Pie Dough for hand pies (page 124)

¼ cup granulated sugar

2 tablespoons raw hazelnuts

¼ cup (½ stick) unsalted butter, melted

2 medium bananas, peeled and sliced ½ inch thick

3 tablespoons light brown sugar

1 teaspoon brandy

¼ cup Nutella

1 large egg beaten with 1 tablespoon water, for egg wash

time will have become fairly soft from handling. Rechilling the butter will prevent the crust from shrinking, make the dough less apt to fall, and create a flakier finished product.)

7. Bake the pies until golden brown, 20 to 25 minutes. Don't overbake, as the filling may break through the seal. Cool on the baking sheet for 30 minutes and serve slightly warm.

8. While these pies are best eaten the day they are baked, you can also wrap them securely and refrigerate; reheat the next day in a 325°F oven for 5 to 8 minutes.

Cherry Amaretto Ricotta Tartlets

½ recipe Flaky Pie Dough for tartlets (page 124)

20 bing cherries, halved and pitted

1 tablespoon plus 1½ teaspoons amaretto or other almond-flavored liqueur, divided

¼ cup plus 1 tablespoon granulated sugar, divided

¾ cup whole milk ricotta

2 teaspoons unbleached all-purpose flour

1 large egg, separated

1 large egg beaten with 1 tablespoon water, for egg wash

2 tablespoons turbinado sugar

Every year in late May or early June, we in the Pacific Northwest cast hopeful eyes toward the fertile fruit-producing country of Eastern Washington. Specifically, we're longing for a delicious bounty of sweet cherries—the first major fruit harvest, signaling the end of a long, dreary winter. This colorful tartlet is by far my favorite way to use fresh cherries—tossed with a little amaretto and combined with sweetened ricotta, then encased in a flaky pastry crust. It's a wonderful way to celebrate the season!

MAKES FOUR 4½-INCH TARTLETS

1. Line a rimmed baking sheet with parchment paper.

2. Remove the dough from the refrigerator and let stand at room temperature for 10 minutes to soften slightly. On a floured work surface, roll the dough out from the center of the disk until it's about ⅛ inch thick. (Check frequently to make sure the dough isn't sticking; add flour as needed to the dough and work surface.) Using a plate, plastic lid, or other object as a guide, cut out four 6½-inch rounds and transfer them to the prepared baking sheet. Store in the refrigerator while you prepare the filling.

3. Toss the cherries with 1 tablespoon of the amaretto and 1 tablespoon of the granulated sugar in a small bowl. Let sit for 20 minutes to macerate (soften and absorb the flavors).

4. Mix the remaining ¼ cup granulated sugar, remaining 1½ teaspoons amaretto, ricotta, flour, and egg yolk thoroughly in a medium bowl. In a separate medium bowl (make sure it's very clean and dry), whip the egg white until it forms medium-stiff peaks using a whisk or hand mixer. Gently fold the egg white into the ricotta mixture; it will have a light, mousselike consistency.

5. Place 5 cherry halves in the center of each dough round and top with ¼ cup of the ricotta mixture, leaving a 1-inch border of dough around the edge. Lift the border up and fold it in, toward the center of the filling, pinching and pleating it securely as you go and brushing the border with the egg wash. (It's very important to seal each pleat thoroughly with egg wash—otherwise, the dough will open up in the baking process.) Continue until you've finished the tartlets; they'll be about 3 inches in diameter. Place 5 cherry halves on top of the ricotta

filling in each tartlet (I like to nestle them pitted side up for a rustic presentation). Sprinkle with the turbinado sugar.

6. Position a rack in the center of the oven and preheat to 350°F.

7. Chill the tartlets in the freezer for 20 minutes. (Don't be tempted to skip this step! The freezer will firm up the dough—which by this time will have become fairly soft from handling. Rechilling the butter will prevent the crust from shrinking and creates a flakier finished product.) At this point the tartlets can be individually wrapped and frozen for up to 2 weeks.

8. Bake the tartlets for 30 to 35 minutes, or until the tops and bottoms are golden brown. The edges will open up a little but shouldn't lose all their pleats. Cool for 20 minutes on the baking sheet and serve slightly warm.

9. These tartlets will keep, wrapped and refrigerated, for 3 days; reheat in a 325°F oven for 10 minutes.

Coconut Cream Tartlets

Here in Seattle, Tom Douglas is a restaurant icon. Perhaps his most renowned creation is a killer coconut cream pie. Our pastry team stepped up recently to create our own Coconut Cream Tartlets—little individual pies—that rival Tom's masterpiece. We use unsweetened coconut in the crust and pastry cream, which also benefits from a generous amount of pure coconut milk. A snowfall of toasted coconut, a fresh raspberry, and a colorful edible flower complete the picture.

NOTE: There are many different tartlet pan sizes and styles, and I encourage you to use what you have. For the quantities in this recipe, however, the ideal size is 4 inches wide.

MAKES SIX 4-INCH TARTLETS

1. To make the tart dough, in the bowl of a stand mixer fitted with the paddle attachment, mix the flour, sugar, and coconut on low speed. Add the butter and mix for 1 to 2 minutes, until the flour is coarse and crumbly. Add the egg all at once and mix just until the dough comes together.

2. Turn dough out onto a piece of plastic wrap. Form the dough into a 1-inch thick block by pulling the sides of the wrap toward the center and patting. Wrap the dough well, then refrigerate until completely chilled, about 2 hours.

3. Meanwhile, to make the custard, mix the sugar, salt, cornstarch, and egg yolks in a medium bowl. I use a stiff wire whisk; the mixture is thick, so it takes a little effort. Set aside.

4. Cook the milk, coconut milk, coconut, and vanilla in a medium saucepan over medium heat, stirring occasionally, and scald the mixture by bringing it just to a boil. Take the pan off the heat. The next step is to temper the hot liquid into the sugar mixture: whisking constantly, pour the hot mixture in a slow stream into the bowl of sugar and yolks. Continue whisking and pouring slowly, until about three-quarters of the milk has been added. Then pour all of the sugar mixture back into the saucepan.

5. Return the saucepan to the burner over low heat and continue whisking to thicken the custard. This will take about 2 minutes: make sure

FOR THE TART DOUGH:

1¼ cups unbleached all-purpose flour

½ cup sugar

½ cup finely shredded unsweetened coconut, toasted (see Toasting Tips, page 7)

½ cup (1 stick) chilled unsalted butter, cut into ¼-inch pieces

1 large egg, beaten

FOR THE COCONUT CUSTARD CREAM:

½ cup sugar

⅛ teaspoon kosher salt

2 tablespoons plus ½ teaspoon cornstarch

3 large egg yolks

½ cup whole milk

1 cup unsweetened coconut milk

½ cup finely shredded unsweetened coconut

1½ teaspoons pure vanilla extract

FOR THE WHIPPED CREAM TOPPING:

1 cup heavy cream

3 tablespoons sugar

1½ teaspoons pure vanilla extract

FOR GARNISH:

½ cup large flake unsweetened coconut, toasted (see Toasting Tips, page 7)

6 fresh raspberries

6 edible flowers, such as Johnny jump-ups or nasturtiums

you are constantly mixing (you don't necessarily have to stir fast, but it's important to be moving the mixture at all times). If the custard sticks to the bottom of the pot and scorches, it will give it a burned taste.

6. Using a rubber spatula, scrape the custard into a medium bowl. Cover with plastic wrap placed directly on the custard's surface and refrigerate until cold, about 2 hours.

7. Position a rack in the center of the oven and preheat to 325°F.

8. Remove the dough from the refrigerator and let stand at room temperature for 10 minutes to soften slightly. On a floured work surface, roll the dough out from the center of the square to about ⅛-inch thickness. (Check frequently to make sure the dough isn't sticking; add flour as needed to the dough and work surface.) Cut out 6 tartlet shells by inverting a tartlet pan onto the dough and cutting a circle slightly larger than its diameter with a paring knife. (This dough is fragile, so handle it with care.) Use an offset spatula to lift each circle into a tartlet pan. Press the dough evenly into the bottom and up the sides of the pans. Trim the outer edge with scissors, or simply use your fingers to pinch the dough off at the pan's edge. Place the pans on a baking sheet and chill for 20 minutes in the freezer.

9. Bake the tartlet shells for 25 to 30 minutes, or until they are deep golden brown. Make sure they are fully baked and not spongy. Cool on the baking sheet for 30 minutes—the shells will continue to firm and crisp as they cool.

10. Meanwhile, to make the topping, in a bowl of a stand mixer fitted with the whisk attachment, whip the heavy cream, sugar, and vanilla on low speed until the cream forms medium-firm peaks. Cover and refrigerate until needed.

11. Pull the custard from the refrigerator and use a rubber spatula to mix and smooth it. Divide it among the tartlet shells; they should be slightly heaping. (I like to use an ice cream scoop.) Using a small offset spatula or the rounded side of a teaspoon, smooth the edges of the custard and form a slight dome in the center. Top each tartlet with an equal volume of whipped cream, smooth, and sprinkle the entire top evenly with toasted coconut. Garnish each with a raspberry and edible flower. Keep chilled until ready to serve. These decadent tartlets will keep, wrapped and refrigerated, for up to 2 days.

Summer Nectarine-Almond Crisp

In my book, the quintessential summer dessert is a freshly baked fruit crisp. While you're making dinner, it can be baking and perfuming your kitchen—creating heady anticipation for the meal ahead. Here, sweet, ripe farmers' market nectarines are tossed with a little sugar, flour, and fresh lemon zest (which nicely balances the fruit's natural sweetness). The topping is an uncomplicated toss of oats, flour, almonds, brown sugar, and butter, baked golden brown and crispy. Served with homemade vanilla ice cream or sweetened whipped cream, or just on its own, it's the perfect ending to a relaxed alfresco summer dinner.

MAKES ONE 9-INCH BAKING DISH

1. Position a rack in the center of the oven and preheat to 375°F. Lightly grease a 9-inch glass baking dish with canola oil.

2. To make the topping, whisk together the flour, oats, almonds, cinnamon, and brown sugar in a medium bowl. Scatter the butter pieces on top, and using a pastry cutter or two forks, cut the butter into the flour mixture until it's coarse and crumbly. Set aside.

3. To prepare the fruit, toss the sugars, flour, and lemon zest in a large bowl. Add the nectarines and almond extract, and toss well. Let sit for 10 minutes to macerate (soften and absorb the flavors).

4. Using a slotted spoon, transfer the nectarines to the prepared baking dish; you will be left with a pool of juice in the bowl. Measure out ¼ cup juice and pour over the nectarines, discarding the rest. Spread the topping evenly over the top of the nectarines.

5. Bake for 40 to 45 minutes, or until the filling is bubbling up around the edges. The juices will look slightly thickened, and the topping will be golden brown. Cool for 45 minutes before serving to set the crisp.

FOR THE TOPPING:

⅓ cup unbleached all-purpose flour

¼ cup thick-cut oats

⅓ cup coarsely chopped raw almonds (skins on)

⅛ teaspoon ground cinnamon

⅓ cup packed light brown sugar

¼ cup (½ stick) chilled unsalted butter, cut into ¼-inch pieces

FOR THE FRUIT:

½ cup granulated sugar

2 tablespoons light brown sugar

2 tablespoons unbleached all-purpose flour

¼ teaspoon lemon zest

7 medium nectarines (about 3 pounds), pitted and cut into ½-inch slices

½ teaspoon pure almond extract

CAKES

CELEBRATIONS OF ALL OCCASIONS—be they grand galas or intimate dinners for two—are always best when accompanied by cake. Its mere mention delights birthday partygoers, and wedding planners prioritize cake for a reason: it's the focal point of the reception (not to mention the subject of highly heated discussions among the bride, groom, and future in-laws).

A cake can be as simple as a quick unfrosted snack baked in a loaf pan or as complicated as a multitiered celebration cake made with mousse, fresh fruit, Italian buttercream, and fondant. This chapter offers a wide variety of recipes.

Along with cupcakes and simple layer cakes are two very elegant, more challenging four-layer cakes: Our Christmas Cassata Cake—composed of lovely orange butter cake, sweetened ricotta, and whipped ganache frosting—is perfect for a holiday gathering or celebration of any kind. And the White Chocolate Whisper Cake is so European in style with its separate layers of fresh raspberries, lemon curd, and sweetened whipped cream.

You'll also find recipes for frostings and fillings that perfectly complement each cake. Frosting doesn't have to be that predictable, toothache-producing mix of powdered sugar and shortening. There's plenty of room for variation, and we've included some standouts, including a recipe that uses pastry cream (the same pudding-like cream that fills a French-style éclair) as the base for a chocolate frosting. Other choices include a cream cheese frosting made with maple syrup, a filling of sweetened ricotta cheese combined with bittersweet chocolate and orange zest, and a simple mix of fresh berries folded with whipped cream.

Cakes *do* take time and planning. But many of their components—frostings, fillings, and flavored syrups—can easily be made in advance. And fresh-baked cake layers, wrapped and frozen, keep well for up to two weeks. When you're ready to assemble your cake, be sure to give our special section, Jane's Step-by-Step Tips for Assembling Beautiful Homemade Cakes, a careful read. Jane Cho, Macrina's talented head pastry chef, has put together these professional tips to set you up for success.

In the end, you needn't worry whether your cakes look like Jane's or not—we all begin by making cakes that look rustic and less than perfect. Let the delight on the faces of those receiving your cake creations power you on with confidence to try more.

Strawberry–Whipped Cream Cupcakes

FOR THE BATTER:

2 cups plus 2 tablespoons cake flour

1½ teaspoons baking powder

½ teaspoon kosher salt

4 large egg yolks

1½ teaspoons pure vanilla extract

½ cup plus 2 tablespoons whole milk, divided

½ cup (1 stick) unsalted butter, at room temperature

1 cup plus 2 tablespoons sugar

FOR THE STRAWBERRY FILLING:

2 cups (about 1½ pints) large fresh strawberries, cut into ¼-inch dice

2 tablespoons good-quality strawberry preserves

FOR THE WHIPPED CREAM:

1½ cups heavy cream

3 tablespoons sugar

1 teaspoon pure vanilla extract

FOR GARNISH:

6 large fresh strawberries, sliced vertically into 4 pieces each, green tops left on

Oh my stars—sweet, deep-red strawberries tossed in fresh strawberry preserves; light, airy, vanilla-scented yellow cake; and sweetened whipped cream. My first memory of a cake like this was at my uncle's wedding in Portland, Oregon. Papa Haydn (the city's longstanding favorite patisserie and café) had prepared a towering confection composed of tiers of golden cake, inches of fresh whipped cream, and fresh Oregon strawberry halves. I can recall it like yesterday because it made such a big impression. This cupcake captures all those wonderful flavors.

MAKES 12 CUPCAKES

1. Position a rack in the center of the oven and preheat to 325°F. Lightly grease the top of a muffin pan with canola oil to prevent any stray batter from sticking, and line 12 cups with standard cupcake liners.

2. To make the batter, sift together the flour, baking powder, and salt in a medium bowl. Set aside.

3. Whisk together the egg yolks, vanilla, and 2 tablespoons of the milk in another medium bowl. Set aside.

4. In the bowl of a stand mixer fitted with the paddle attachment or in a medium bowl using an electric mixer, cream the butter and sugar. Start on low speed and increase to medium for a total of 5 to 8 minutes, stopping to scrape down the bowl with a rubber spatula as needed to fully incorporate ingredients. The mixture will be light, fluffy, and pale. Add the dry ingredients and the remaining ½ cup milk, alternating in 2 additions and stopping occasionally to scrape down the bowl. Mix for another 20 seconds. Add the egg mixture in 3 additions, mixing for 20 seconds each time, again stopping occasionally to scrape down the bowl.

5. With a large spoon or #30 ice cream scoop, fill the cupcake liners three-quarters full with batter. Smooth the tops for even baking. Place the pan on a rimmed baking sheet and bake for 30 to 35 minutes, or until the cupcakes are golden brown and a skewer inserted into the center comes out clean. Halfway through baking, check the cupcakes: if they are browning unevenly, rotate the pan. Cool them in the pan for 20 minutes, then carefully transfer to a wire rack to cool completely.

6. To make the strawberry filling, toss the strawberries with the preserves in a small bowl. Set aside.

7. To make the whipped cream, in a bowl of a stand mixer fitted with the whisk attachment, whip the cream, sugar, and vanilla, starting on low speed and increasing gradually, until the cream forms medium-stiff peaks.

8. To assemble, use a teaspoon to scoop out a 1-inch ball from the center of each cupcake. Discard (or eat!) the cake and fill the hole with the strawberry mixture, leveling the top. Top with a generous dollop of whipped cream. I like to use an ice cream scoop to distribute and sculpt the whipped cream, gently rotating the back of the scoop in a circular motion to create a swirl. You can get a different look by using a small offset spatula to level the top and straighten the sides. Garnish each cupcake with 2 strawberry pieces.

Cupid's Red Velvet Cupcakes

FOR THE BATTER:

1½ cups unbleached all-purpose flour

2 tablespoons Dutch-process cocoa powder

1½ teaspoons baking soda

½ teaspoon kosher salt

½ cup buttermilk

1 teaspoon pure vanilla extract

1½ teaspoons red food coloring

1 tablespoon water

1 teaspoon white wine vinegar

¼ cup (½ stick) unsalted butter, at room temperature

⅓ cup canola oil

¾ cup plus 1 tablespoon granulated sugar

1 large egg

FOR THE WHITE CHOCOLATE FROSTING:

¾ cup white chocolate chips

6 ounces (¾ cup) cream cheese, at room temperature

6 tablespoons (¾ stick) unsalted butter, at room temperature

1 teaspoon freshly squeezed lemon juice

FOR GARNISH:

10 edible rose petals

2 tablespoons confectioners' sugar

This popular cake came from a pastry chef at New York City's Waldorf Astoria hotel. Its unusual red color was thought to be caused by a chemical reaction between the baking soda and cocoa powder. Truth be told, to achieve the distinctive color associated with red velvet cake, you'll need a secret ingredient: red food coloring. I've tried natural alternatives such as dried beet powder, but they tend to bake out light brown or mauve. This version uses a minimum amount of food coloring, so you can enjoy the lovely red hue while focusing your palate on its sweet cocoa and butter overtones.

NOTE: If you want to create a special presentation for your cupcakes, look for colorful and festive cupcake holders. Just drop your decorated cupcakes in, then either reuse the holders or give them as gifts along with the cupcakes.

MAKES 10 CUPCAKES

1. Position a rack in the center of the oven and preheat to 350°F. Lightly grease the top of a cupcake pan with canola oil to prevent any stray batter from sticking, and line 10 cups with standard cupcake liners.

2. To make the batter, sift together the flour, cocoa powder, baking soda, and salt in a medium bowl. Set aside.

3. Whisk together the buttermilk, vanilla, food coloring, water, and vinegar in another medium bowl. Set aside.

4. In the bowl of a stand mixer fitted with the paddle attachment, cream the butter, canola oil, and granulated sugar. Start on low speed and increase to medium for a total of 5 to 8 minutes, stopping to scrape down the bowl with a rubber spatula as needed to fully incorporate ingredients. The mixture will be light, fluffy, and pale. Add the egg, mix thoroughly, and scrape down the bowl again. With the mixer on low speed, add the dry ingredients in 3 additions, alternating with the buttermilk mixture in 2 additions, blending just until incorporated. Scrape down the bowl again and mix for another 20 seconds on medium speed.

5. Using a large spoon or #30 ice cream scoop, fill the cupcake liners three-quarters full with batter. Smooth the tops for even baking. Place

the pan on a rimmed baking sheet and bake for 25 to 30 minutes, or until the cupcakes are deep brown and a skewer inserted into the center comes out clean. Halfway through baking, check the cupcakes: if they are browning unevenly, rotate the pan. Cool them in the pan for 20 minutes, then carefully transfer to a wire rack to cool completely.

6. Meanwhile, to make the frosting, melt the white chocolate chips over medium heat in a double boiler or a stainless steel bowl set over a small saucepan filled with about 2 inches of water. (The bowl should not touch the water.) Bring the water to a simmer and, using a spatula, stir the chips to help them melt evenly. When the chocolate has completely melted, remove the bowl and set aside to cool for 5 minutes.

7. In the bowl of a stand mixer fitted with the paddle attachment, mix the cream cheese and butter, starting on low speed and increasing to medium, for a total of 5 to 8 minutes, stopping to scrape the bowl as needed. (Your goal is to fully aerate the mixture and remove any lumps; cream cheese is notoriously difficult to smooth out.) Add the lemon juice and mix briefly. With the mixer on low speed, drizzle in the warm chocolate; scrape down the bowl to make sure everything is well incorporated. Mix for an additional 1 to 2 minutes to add volume to the frosting. (If you still see lumps of white chocolate in the frosting, you can warm the bowl over the water bath for 30 seconds and stir, or push the frosting through a sieve to remove the lumps.)

8. To assemble, use a spoon or #30 ice cream scoop to place a 1¾-inch ball of frosting atop each cupcake. With a small offset spatula or the back of a spoon, level the frosting and then push it, pressing lightly, in a circular direction, starting on the rim of the cupcake and finishing in the center. This creates a pretty swirl design. Garnish the center of each cupcake with a rose petal and dust lightly with confectioners' sugar.

Gluten-Free Banana Cupcakes with Chocolate Cream Frosting

FOR THE BATTER:

¾ cup mashed ripe bananas (about 1½ medium)

¼ cup sour cream

1 large egg

1½ teaspoons lemon zest (from 1 large lemon)

1 teaspoon pure vanilla extract

1 cup plus 2 tablespoons gluten-free flour mix (such as Bob's Red Mill or King Arthur, found in most major grocery stores)

¾ teaspoon baking soda

½ teaspoon baking powder

¼ teaspoon kosher salt

¼ teaspoon xanthan gum

½ cup (1 stick) unsalted butter, at room temperature

½ cup plus 2 tablespoons sugar

FOR THE CHOCOLATE CREAM FROSTING:

1 cup good-quality semisweet chocolate chips

½ cup whole milk

¾ cup heavy cream

3 tablespoons sugar

1 teaspoon pure vanilla extract

There's no doubt that at some point you've asked yourself the question, "What are we going to do with these ripe bananas?" Banana bread is the common answer, but why not try something different—these cupcakes may become your new favorite treat! Made with a gluten-free flour blend, a few ripe bananas, sour cream, butter, and sugar, they're topped with a dollop of light chocolate whipped cream. You can decorate them with colorful sprinkles, clear decorating sugar, edible flowers, or even dried, sugared banana chips—or my favorite, dark chocolate curls.

MAKES 12 CUPCAKES

1. Position a rack in the center of the oven and preheat to 325°F. Lightly grease the top of a muffin pan with canola oil to prevent any stray batter from sticking, and line 12 cups with standard cupcake liners.

2. To make the batter, combine the bananas, sour cream, egg, lemon zest, and vanilla in a medium bowl. Set aside.

3. Sift together the flour mix, baking soda, baking powder, salt, and xanthan gum in a separate medium bowl. Set aside.

4. In the bowl of a stand mixer fitted with the paddle attachment, cream the butter and sugar. Start on low speed and increase to medium for a total of 5 to 8 minutes, stopping to scrape down the bowl with a rubber spatula as needed to fully incorporate ingredients. The mixture will be light, fluffy, and pale. Add the flour mixture and half of the banana mixture, mix for 1½ minutes, and scrape down the bowl again. Add the remaining banana mixture in 2 additions, mixing for 20 seconds each time and scraping down the bowl between additions.

5. Using a large spoon or #30 ice cream scoop, fill the cupcake liners three-quarters full with batter. Smooth the tops for even baking. Place the pan on a rimmed baking sheet and bake for 25 to 30 minutes, or until the cupcakes are deep golden brown and a skewer inserted into the center comes out clean. (Note that these cupcakes will rise only to the top of the pan as they bake.) Cool in the pan for 20 minutes, then carefully transfer to a wire rack to cool completely.

6. Meanwhile, to make the frosting, melt the chocolate chips with the milk over medium-low heat in a medium bowl set over a saucepan filled with about 2 inches of water. (The bowl should not touch the water.) This will act as a water bath to gently melt the chocolate without scorching. Using a rubber spatula, stir the mixture slowly until the chocolate has completely melted. Remove the bowl and set aside to cool to room temperature, about 20 minutes.

7. In the bowl of a stand mixer fitted with the whisk attachment, whip the heavy cream, sugar, and vanilla until they form medium-stiff peaks. Using a rubber spatula, fold the whipped cream into the chocolate mixture in 3 or 4 additions, folding gently each time. Your goal is to blend the two elements without deflating the cream. Cover the frosting with plastic wrap and refrigerate for about 1 hour to set up.

8. To assemble, use a spoon or #30 ice cream scoop to place a generous dollop of frosting atop each cupcake. With a small offset spatula or the back of a spoon, level the frosting and then push it, pressing lightly, in a circular direction, starting on the rim of the cupcake and finishing in the center. Decorate as desired.

Almond Cake with Raspberries and Chocolate Ganache

This combination of toasted almonds in a buttery cake, accompanied by fresh raspberries and bittersweet chocolate ganache, is our best-selling wedding cake. It satisfies everyone's taste with nuts, fruit, and of course, chocolate. This recipe makes individually sized cakes that are baked in a jumbo muffin pan. Once they've cooled, you remove the paper liner, invert the cakes so the tapered side is up, fill with sweetened cream and raspberries, and top with the chocolate ganache.

MAKES 8 JUMBO CUPCAKES

1. Position a rack in the center of the oven and preheat to 400°F. Lightly grease the top of a jumbo muffin pan with canola oil to prevent any stray batter from sticking, and line 8 cups with jumbo cupcake liners.

2. To make the batter, first grind the toasted almonds in a food processor until they are very fine and powdery. (Alternatively, grind them by hand: chop the nuts as finely as you can with a chef's knife, then use the flat side of the knife to crush the chopped nuts into a powder.) Sift together the flour, baking powder, baking soda, and salt in a medium bowl. Add the almonds and toss with your hands to evenly distribute. Set aside.

3. Whisk 2 tablespoons of the yogurt, eggs, and almond and vanilla extracts in a small bowl. Set aside.

4. In the bowl of a stand mixer fitted with the paddle attachment, cream the butter and sugar; start on low speed and increase to medium, stopping to scrape down the bowl with a rubber spatula as needed to fully incorporate the ingredients. The mixture will be light, fluffy, and pale. Add the flour mixture and the remaining ½ cup yogurt, slowly mixing for 1 minute. Once the flour is incorporated, increase to medium speed and mix for 1 minute more, then scrape down the bowl again. Add the egg mixture in 3 additions, mixing for 20 seconds after each addition, then scraping down the bowl.

5. Using a large spoon or #30 ice cream scoop, fill the cupcake liners three-quarters full with batter. Smooth the tops for even baking. Place the pan on a rimmed baking sheet and bake for 30 minutes, or until the cupcakes are deep golden brown and a skewer inserted into the center

FOR THE BATTER:

½ cup raw almonds (skins on), toasted (see Toasting Tips, page 7)

1½ cups cake flour

½ teaspoon baking powder

½ teaspoon baking soda

¼ teaspoon kosher salt

½ cup plus 2 tablespoons low-fat plain yogurt, divided

2 large eggs

½ teaspoon pure almond extract

¼ teaspoon pure vanilla extract

¾ cup (1½ sticks) unsalted butter

1 cup plus 2 tablespoons sugar

FOR THE WHIPPED CREAM FILLING:

1 pint fresh raspberries (about 24 berries)

½ cup heavy cream

2 tablespoons sugar

FOR THE CHOCOLATE GANACHE:

½ cup heavy cream

½ cup semisweet chocolate chips

½ cup bittersweet chocolate chips

comes out clean. (Note that these cupcakes will rise only to the top of the muffin pan as they bake.) Cool them in the pan for 45 minutes, then remove them and peel off the cupcake liners. Invert the cakes onto a plate so the bottoms are up and using a teaspoon, scoop out a 1½-inch ball from the center of each cake and discard (or eat!) the cake.

6. To make the filling, pick through the raspberries, reserving 8 beauties for garnish. Whisk the heavy cream and sugar in a small bowl, whipping until they form medium-firm peaks, then fold in the raspberries. You want the berries to break up a bit—but don't let them get soupy. Spoon the raspberry whipped cream into the hole in the cakes, piling in as much as you can and leveling the top.

7. To make the ganache, pour the heavy cream into a small saucepan. Over medium heat bring the cream to a froth just before it boils. Turn off the heat and add the semisweet and bittersweet chocolate chips. Using a rubber spatula, stir until the chocolate completely melts, then remove the pan from the heat and set aside to cool for about 10 minutes. The ganache will thicken as it cools.

8. To assemble, top each cake with 1 tablespoon of the ganache; spread it evenly, but leave a little of the golden cake showing around the edges. Garnish with a raspberry.

9. These cakes taste best the day they are made. You can prepare them up to the point of making the filling and store, covered, at room temperature for 2 days.

Fourth of July Buttermilk Cake

This delicious cake makes its appearance each year around the Fourth of July; it's a perfect picnic treat. Sweet yet tangy buttermilk cake layers combined with an ultracreamy milk chocolate buttercream frosting make it truly special. The frosting starts with pastry cream, a thickened, egg yolk-based custard that adds richness and stability; then chocolate and butter are added for a luscious finish. Finally, we brush almond syrup on the cake layers, which provides even more moistness and flavor. I like to garnish this cake with a small bouquet of edible flowers or seasonal fruit and a dusting of confectioners' sugar.

MAKES ONE 9-INCH CAKE

1. Position a rack in the center of the oven and preheat to 325°F. Lightly brush two 9-inch round cake pans with canola oil. Cut out two 8-inch parchment paper squares and place them on the bottom of the pans to prevent the cakes from sticking. Line a wire cooling rack with parchment paper.

2. To make the batter, sift together the flour, baking powder, baking soda, and salt in a medium bowl. Set aside.

3. Combine the buttermilk and vanilla in a small bowl. Set aside.

4. In the bowl of a stand mixer fitted with the paddle attachment, cream the butter and granulated sugar; start on low speed and increase to medium for a total of 5 to 8 minutes, stopping to scrape down the bowl with a rubber spatula as needed to fully incorporate the ingredients. The mixture will be light, fluffy, and pale. Add the eggs one at a time, mixing until each egg is fully incorporated before adding the next one and scraping down the bowl between additions.

5. With the mixer on low speed, add the flour mixture in 3 additions, alternating with the buttermilk mixture in 2 additions, blending just until incorporated. Scrape down the bowl again and mix for another 20 seconds on medium speed to add air and volume to the cake batter.

6. Divide the batter between the 2 prepared pans; they will be about two-thirds full. Using an offset spatula, smooth and level the batter for even baking. Bake for 25 minutes, then reduce the oven temperature to 300°F and bake for another 15 minutes, or until the cakes are deep golden brown and a skewer inserted into the center comes out clean.

FOR THE BATTER:

2½ cups unbleached all-purpose flour

1¾ teaspoons baking powder

¼ teaspoon baking soda

¼ teaspoon kosher salt

¾ cups buttermilk

¾ teaspoon pure vanilla extract

¾ cup (1½ sticks) unsalted butter, at room temperature

1½ cups plus 2 tablespoons granulated sugar

3 large eggs

FOR THE BUTTERCREAM FROSTING:

1 cup confectioners' sugar, divided

3 large egg yolks

1 tablespoon plus 1 teaspoon unbleached all-purpose flour

Pinch of kosher salt

⅔ cup whole milk

1½ cups good-quality milk chocolate chips

2 ounces unsweetened chocolate, coarsely chopped

1 teaspoon pure vanilla extract

1½ cups (3 sticks) unsalted butter, cut into tablespoons, at room temperature

FOR THE ALMOND SYRUP:

½ cup water

⅓ cup granulated sugar

½ teaspoon pure almond extract

½ teaspoon pure vanilla extract

7. Cool the cakes in the pans for 30 minutes. Run a knife around the sides of the pans and invert the cakes onto the prepared rack. Carefully remove the paper and cool completely.

8. Meanwhile, to make the frosting, sift ¼ cup of the confectioners' sugar into a small bowl. Add the egg yolks, flour, and salt and whisk thoroughly to remove any lumps; set aside. In a small saucepan over medium-low heat, bring the milk to a froth just before it boils. Pour a few dribbles of the hot milk into the yolk mixture, whisking constantly, then slowly add more until it has all been incorporated. Now pour it all back into the saucepan and continue cooking the custard over low heat, taking care to whisk constantly (this is a small amount and will scorch easily). This custard thickens quickly, in 1 to 2 minutes. Using a rubber spatula, press the custard through a strainer and into a small bowl to remove any lumps. Press a piece of plastic wrap onto the custard's surface. Chill in the refrigerator for about 45 minutes, until it has cooled enough to set up.

9. Melt the chocolate chips with the unsweetened chocolate over medium heat in a double boiler or a stainless steel bowl set over a small saucepan filled with about 2 inches of water. (The bowl should not touch the water.) This will act as a water bath to gently melt the chocolate without scorching. Using a rubber spatula, stir the mixture slowly to help the chocolate melt evenly. When the chocolate has completely melted, remove the bowl and set aside to cool to room temperature, about 15 minutes.

10. Sift the remaining ¾ cup confectioners' sugar into a small bowl. In the bowl of a stand mixer fitted with the paddle attachment, mix the chilled custard on low speed to smooth it. Add the sifted sugar gradually, along with the vanilla. Add the soft butter several pieces at a time, mixing with each addition. When all the butter has been incorporated, mix for another minute or so, until the mixture is very smooth. With the mixer on low speed, add the chocolate gradually in a slow stream. Scrape down the bowl and mix for 20 more seconds to make sure the chocolate is fully incorporated and there are no streaks. Hold the frosting at room temperature until ready to use.

11. To make the almond syrup, whisk the water and granulated sugar in a small saucepan until the sugar has dissolved. Bring to a simmer over medium heat and cook for 3 to 5 minutes, until the liquid has reduced by a third. Remove the pan from the heat and whisk in the almond and vanilla extracts. Set aside.

12. To assemble (see Jane's Step-by-Step Tips for Assembling Beautiful Homemade Cakes, page 161), trim the sides, top, and bottom of the cakes with a serrated knife, removing any dark edges and leveling the domed tops. Place one cake on a plate or cardboard cake round. Lightly brush it with about half of the almond syrup. Place 1½ cups frosting in the center of the cake and spread evenly, leaving a 1-inch unfrosted border around the edge; the frosting will be about ⅜ inch thick. Set the other cake on top and level by gently pressing down on it with the bottom of an empty cake pan. Brush with the remaining almond syrup.

13. Cover the entire cake with a thin layer of frosting about ⅛ inch thick. This is the crumb coat, so the cake will still be visible through the frosting. Refrigerate the cake for 20 minutes to firm it up, holding the remaining frosting at room temperature.

14. For the final coat, use a layer of frosting no more than ¼ inch thick. First cover the sides of the cake; the frosting should be evenly distributed on the offset spatula so that you can coat the sides (top to bottom) all at once. Then frost the top, placing a dollop of frosting in the center and smoothing it out, squaring up the edges.

15. Store the frosted cake, wrapped well, in the refrigerator for up to 4 days. Bring it to room temperature (about 2 hours) before serving.

* Jane's Step-*by*-Step Tips *for* Assembling Beautiful Homemade Cakes *

Cake assembly can be intimidating—mostly because it's not something home bakers have the chance to perfect day after day. Our head pastry chef, Jane Cho, started with us back in 2005 with limited experience but lots of enthusiasm, determination, and natural talent. She was undaunted by all there was to learn—and within a year her cakes and pastries were show-stoppers. In the time Jane has been with us, she's built a great deal of confidence in her craft and has become a teacher and mentor to many of our bakers and employees. She's a natural problem solver, has an ultra-artistic eye for detail, and is an extremely talented pastry technician. How grateful we are to have Jane as part of the Macrina family.

Here are a few tips from pastry chef Jane Cho to sharpen your skills—and ease anxiety—while assembling layer cakes.

NOTE: If you have the desire to sharpen your cake assembly skills, put aside the fancy gadgets and purchase a cake-decorating turntable and two offset spatulas (see Kitchen Must-Haves, page xix). These two culinary tools will get you miles down the road to making beautiful homemade cakes—and make it much more fun to practice!

1. For light-colored cake layers, trim a thin "skin" from the top, sides, and bottom of the freshly baked cake (using a serrated knife), revealing the consistent color beneath. While you're at it, slice off any domed tops so that the layers are flat.

2. If your cake is fragile, as freshly baked cakes often are, chill the layers in the freezer for 20 minutes before cutting or moving; they will be easier to handle.

3. To cut multiple layers from a single cake, start by placing the cake on a turntable or plate, then holding the serrated knife parallel to your work surface at the level you want to split the cake. Place your other hand on top of the cake.

Gently turn the cake with that hand, keeping the knife still and level. The goal is to create a ½-inch cut into the cake all the way around. Now repeat that motion, slipping the knife into the cut you just made, and continuing to rotate the cake on the turntable. Apply slight pressure with your knife while keeping it level; the knife will make its way through the cake. Using the flat bottom of a tart pan or a cardboard cake round, lift the top layer onto a piece of parchment.

4. When filling a cake, start by using your offset spatula to indent the top of the cake slightly, tracing a line around it about 1 inch from the edge. Place a dollop of frosting in the center of the layer. Then, applying slight pressure to the filling with your spatula, spin the turntable, leaving your spatula centered on the cake; the filling will spread outward. Leave the 1-inch border at the edge of the cake unfrosted. Check to see that the filling is level.

5. Set the next cake layer on top of the filling, then gently press down on the layer so that it pushes the filling toward the unfrosted edge and helps the layers adhere to one another. (Don't worry if some gaps remain around the cake's edge—your crumb coat will "grab" the

frosting later and fill them in.) Spin the cake around and adjust as necessary to see that the layers are stable and level. If your cake feels fragile, chill it in the freezer for 20 minutes.

6. The next step, crumb coating, is one you don't want to skip. It's the process of coating the entire cake with a very thin layer of frosting before applying the final coat. It seals in the fillings and glues any loose crumbs in place so they don't mar the look of the finished cake. Start with the sides: the frosting should be evenly distributed on the offset spatula so you can coat from top to bottom all at once, spreading a layer no more than ⅛ inch thick. Finish by spreading the crumb coat evenly over the top of the cake and squaring up the edges.

7. For the final coat of frosting, start with the sides first, then do the top. Again, to ensure straight sides, the frosting should be evenly distributed on the offset spatula so you can coat the sides all at once. Cleaning your spatula occasionally of excess frosting will produce a smoother finish coat. It's also helpful when spreading thicker frostings and smoothing any rough edges or lines to warm the spatula; do this by running it under hot water, then quickly wiping it dry.

8. Your cake is almost finished! You may want to chill it briefly to help the frosting set completely. After about 20 minutes in the freezer, use a bench knife to gently scrape off a *very* thin layer from the sides, removing any imperfections. Using a dry offset spatula, do the same with the top. When you're happy with the overall look of your cake, add any additional decorations. Possibilities include adding piped edges and frills (using your finishing frosting), streaking the top with melted chocolate, or adding fresh fruit, nuts, edible flowers, colored sugar, or chocolate curls. Even the simplest additions will give your cake a special individual touch.

Apple Autumn Cake with Maple Cream Cheese Frosting

This gem of a cake bursts with sweet spices, tart apples, currants, brandy, toasted walnuts, and molasses. The layers are frosted with a caramel-like, maple cream cheese frosting, and its lovely rustic appearance shows off the cake itself with no frosting sealing up the sides. This cake is a baker's dream because—due to the extra moistness provided by the apples and the way a little time helps the spice flavors to meld—it actually improves in the days following baking.

MAKES ONE 9-INCH CAKE

1. Position a rack in the center of the oven and preheat to 325°F. Lightly grease two 9-inch round cake pans with canola oil. Cut out two 8-inch parchment paper squares and place them on the bottom of the pans to prevent the cakes from sticking. Line a wire cooling rack with parchment paper. Set aside.

2. To make the batter, soak the currants in a medium bowl filled with hot water to cover for 20 minutes. Drain off any excess water, add the walnuts and apples, and toss to combine. Set aside.

3. Sift together the flour, baking soda, cinnamon, nutmeg, cloves, and salt in a medium bowl. Set aside.

4. In the bowl of a stand mixer fitted with the paddle attachment, mix the butter, granulated sugar, brandy, and vanilla on low speed for 5 to 8 minutes, scraping down the bowl as needed, until the mixture is light and pale. Add the eggs one at a time, mixing until each egg is fully incorporated before adding the next. Using a rubber spatula, scrape down the bowl to fully incorporate the ingredients. Add the molasses and fresh ginger and continue mixing for another 30 seconds.

5. Remove the bowl from the mixer and, using a rubber spatula, add the flour and apple mixtures in 4 alternating additions, folding the ingredients completely but gently with each addition. (It may seem a little tedious, but adding the ingredients a little at a time helps avoid overmixing the batter, which can result in a tough cake.)

FOR THE BATTER:

1 cup dried currants

1 cup raw walnuts, toasted (see Toasting Tips, page 7) and coarsely chopped

3 medium Granny Smith apples, peeled, cored, and cut into ½-inch dice

2½ cups unbleached all-purpose flour

2 teaspoons baking soda

1½ teaspoons ground cinnamon

¼ teaspoon freshly grated nutmeg

¼ teaspoon ground cloves

½ teaspoon kosher salt

1 cup (2 sticks) unsalted butter, at room temperature

2¼ cups granulated sugar

1 tablespoon brandy

1½ teaspoons pure vanilla extract

4 large eggs

2 tablespoons molasses

½ teaspoon peeled, grated fresh ginger

FOR THE MAPLE CREAM CHEESE FROSTING:

1 cup confectioners' sugar

8 ounces (1 cup) cream cheese, at room temperature

½ cup (1 stick) unsalted butter, at room temperature

¼ cup pure maple syrup

FOR GARNISH:

2 pieces crystallized ginger, slivered

1 tablespoon dried currants

6. Divide the batter between the 2 prepared pans; it will fill them about ¼ inch from the top (the cakes will not rise very much). Using an offset spatula, smooth and level the batter for even baking. Bake for 45 to 50 minutes, or until the cakes are deep brown and a skewer inserted into the center comes out clean. Cool the cakes in the pans for 20 minutes. Run a knife around the sides of the pans and invert the cakes onto the prepared rack. Carefully remove the paper and cool completely.

7. Meanwhile, to make the frosting, sift the confectioners' sugar into a small bowl. In the bowl of a stand mixer fitted with the paddle attachment, mix the cream cheese and butter on low speed for 2 to 3 minutes to remove any lumps. Add the confectioners' sugar and mix on low speed to incorporate, then pour the maple syrup in gradually. Increase to medium speed and mix for 2 to 3 minutes more to thoroughly smooth and aerate the frosting. Keep at room temperature until ready to use.

8. To assemble (see Jane's Step-by-Step Tips for Assembling Beautiful Homemade Cakes, page 161), place one cake on a plate or cardboard cake round. Place 1½ cups of frosting in the center of the cake and spread evenly, leaving a 1-inch unfrosted border around the edge. Set the other cake on top and level by gently pressing down on it with the bottom of an empty cake pan. Spread the remainder of the frosting over the top layer, leveling it all the way to the edge. (For a fancier presentation, put the remaining frosting in a pastry bag with a star tip. Pipe concentric circles on the cake, starting along the edge and finishing in the center. Smooth out the center portion, but leave half the outside row of piping intact. This pulls the bead slightly inward so the frosting looks like a ruffle along the rim of the cake. See photo, opposite) Garnish by arranging the crystallized ginger attractively in the center of the cake, and scattering the dried currants over. (Sugared cranberries and rosemary also make a nice garnish.)

9. Store the frosted cake, well wrapped, in the refrigerator for up to 1 week. Bring it to room temperature (about 2 hours) before serving.

Macrina's Carrot Cake

FOR THE BATTER:

¾ cup walnut halves and pieces, toasted (see Toasting Tips, page 7) and finely chopped

2¼ cups packed grated carrots (5 to 6 medium), divided

2¼ cups unbleached all-purpose flour

1½ teaspoons baking powder

1½ teaspoons baking soda

½ teaspoon kosher salt

2 teaspoons ground cinnamon

½ teaspoon freshly grated nutmeg

⅛ teaspoon ground cloves

¾ cup canola oil

1¾ cups plus 2 tablespoons granulated sugar, divided

3 large eggs

½ cup applesauce (preferably organic)

1 tablespoon orange zest (from 1 orange)

3 or 4 edible flowers, for garnish

FOR THE FROSTING:

1 pound (2 cups) cream cheese, at room temperature

¾ cup (1½ sticks) unsalted butter, at room temperature

1¾ cups confectioners' sugar

1 teaspoon freshly squeezed lemon juice

Why does absolutely everyone love carrot cake? Could it be the loads of freshly grated carrots and toasted walnuts, providing nutrition and sustenance? Maybe it's the distinctive moist, sweet cake itself. Or is it the undeniably perfect complement of cream cheese frosting? I think it's all of the above. This recipe makes an elegant two-layer cake; it can also be made into cupcakes or a single layer cake baked in a rectangular baking pan. Whichever shape you choose, this cake is especially easy to mix because it uses canola oil instead of butter, and it's extra moist with the addition of applesauce.

MAKES ONE 9-INCH CAKE

1. Position a rack in the center of the oven and preheat to 325°F. Lightly grease two 9-inch round cake pans with canola oil. Cut out two 8-inch parchment paper squares and place them on the bottom of the pans to prevent the cakes from sticking. Line a wire cooling rack and a baking sheet with parchment paper. Set aside.

2. To make the batter, toss the walnuts with 2 cups of the grated carrots in a large bowl. Set aside.

3. Sift together the flour, baking powder, baking soda, salt, cinnamon, nutmeg, and cloves in a medium bowl. Set aside.

4. In the bowl of a stand mixer fitted with the paddle attachment, mix the canola oil, 1¾ cups of the granulated sugar, eggs, and applesauce. Start on low speed and increase to medium for a total of 3 to 5 minutes, until the mixture is lighter in texture and slightly lighter in color. Scrape down the bowl with a rubber spatula to fully incorporate the ingredients. With the mixer on low speed, add the flour mixture and incorporate it fairly quickly (about 20 seconds), then scrape down the bowl again. Remove the bowl from the mixer and use the rubber spatula to fold in the carrot mixture.

5. Divide the batter between the 2 prepared pans; they will be about two-thirds full. Using an offset spatula, smooth and level the batter for even baking. Bake for 35 or 40 minutes, or until the cakes are deep golden brown and a skewer inserted into the center comes out clean. Cool the cakes in the pans for 20 minutes. Run a knife around the sides of the pans and invert the cakes onto the prepared rack. Carefully remove the paper and cool completely.

6. Meanwhile, to make the frosting, in the bowl of a stand mixer fitted with the paddle attachment, mix the cream cheese and butter for 5 minutes on medium speed to thoroughly smooth and aerate the frosting. Sift the confectioners' sugar into a medium bowl and gradually add it to the cream cheese mixture. Add the lemon juice and mix for another 2 minutes, until the frosting is smooth and light. Hold it at room temperature until ready to use. (If it seems too warm and loose to hold its shape, refrigerate it, checking every 5 minutes and mixing with a rubber spatula until it looks spreadable.)

7. Spread the remaining ¼ cup carrots on the prepared baking sheet in a single layer. Bake for 3 minutes to slightly dry them out, then toss with the remaining 2 tablespoons granulated sugar. Bake for another 8 to 10 minutes, until the carrots are crisp but not browned. (As they cool they will crisp up more.) Set aside to cool.

8. To assemble (see Jane's Step-by-Step Tips for Assembling Beautiful Homemade Cakes, page 161), trim the top of the cakes with a serrated knife, leveling the domed tops. Place one cake cut side up on a plate or cardboard cake round. Place 1½ cups of frosting in the center of the cake and spread evenly, leaving a 1-inch unfrosted border around the edge; the frosting will be about ⅜ inch thick. Sprinkle the orange zest over the frosting. Set the other cake on top and level by gently pressing down on it with the bottom of an empty cake pan.

9. Cover the entire cake with a thin layer of frosting about ⅛ inch thick. This is the crumb coat, so the cake will still be visible through the frosting. Refrigerate the cake for 20 minutes to firm it up, holding the remaining frosting at room temperature.

10. For the final coat use a layer of frosting no more than ¼ inch thick. First cover the sides of the cake; the frosting should be evenly distributed on the offset spatula so that you can coat the sides (top to bottom) all at once. Then frost the top, placing a dollop of frosting in the center and smoothing it out, squaring up the edges. Garnish by placing a 4-inch ring of baked carrots in the center of the cake and fill with the edible flowers.

11. You can store the baked cakes, unfrosted and well wrapped, in the freezer for up to 2 weeks. The frosted cake can be refrigerated for up to 4 days. Bring it to room temperature (about 2 hours) before serving.

White Chocolate Whisper Cake

This recipe was inspired by Rose Levy Beranbaum's fabulous Cake Bible cookbook. Years ago, when customers started asking for specialty cakes, it became our source of inspiration. We've mostly retired this treasured book, now tattered and worn, but many of the cakes we made from it live on, including this ever-popular, elegant Whisper Cake. A fellow soccer mom hailed me at a game recently and told me about her memories of eating it on her fortieth birthday. She recalled its layers of tangy lemon curd, sweetened whipped cream, and fresh raspberries, and the perfectly balanced white chocolate–cream cheese frosting. She's about to celebrate her 50th birthday and is hankering for an encore!

NOTE: The cake layers can be baked, wrapped tightly, and frozen for up to 2 weeks ahead; thaw them before assembling. The lemon curd may be made up to 3 days in advance and stored, tightly covered, in the refrigerator. The lemon syrup can be made several days ahead and held in the refrigerator as well. The frosting can be made up to a week in advance, but must be brought to room temperature and rewhipped before using.

MAKES ONE 9-INCH CAKE

1. Position a rack in the center of the oven and preheat to 325°F. Lightly grease two 9-inch round cake pans with canola oil. Cut out two 8-inch parchment paper squares and place them on the bottom of the pans to prevent the cakes from sticking. Line a wire cooling rack with parchment paper. Set aside.

2. To make the batter, melt the white chocolate chips with the canola oil in a double boiler or a stainless steel bowl set over a saucepan filled with about 2 inches of water. (The bowl should not touch the water.) This will act as a water bath to gently melt the chocolate without scorching. Using a rubber spatula, stir the mixture slowly to help the chocolate melt evenly. When the chocolate has completely melted, remove the bowl and set aside to cool to room temperature, about 20 minutes.

3. Sift together the flour, baking powder, and salt in a medium bowl. Set aside.

4. Whisk the egg whites, vanilla, and ¼ cup of the milk in a small bowl; the mixture should be homogenous but not frothy. Set aside.

FOR THE BATTER:

¾ cup good-quality white chocolate chips

1 teaspoon canola oil

2½ cups cake flour

1 tablespoon plus 1 teaspoon baking powder

½ teaspoon kosher salt

4 large egg whites (save the yolks for the lemon curd)

1½ teaspoons pure vanilla extract

¾ cup plus 1 tablespoon whole milk, divided

½ cup (1 stick) unsalted butter, at room temperature

1¼ cups sugar

FOR THE WHIPPED CREAM:

¾ cup heavy cream

¼ cup sugar

FOR THE LEMON SYRUP:

½ cup water

⅓ cup sugar

¼ cup freshly squeezed lemon juice (from about 1 large lemon)

FOR THE LEMON CURD:

6 large egg yolks

1 cup sugar

⅔ cup freshly squeezed lemon juice (from about 3 large lemons)

6 tablespoons (¾ stick) unsalted butter, cut into tablespoons, at room temperature

continued

FOR THE WHITE CHOCOLATE–CREAM CHEESE FROSTING:

12 ounces good-quality white chocolate chips

2 teaspoons canola oil

1 pound (2 cups) cream cheese, at room temperature

1 cup (2 sticks) unsalted butter, at room temperature

2 tablespoons freshly squeezed lemon juice

FOR THE RASPBERRY FILLING:

½ cup good-quality raspberry preserves

2 cups (1 pint) fresh raspberries

5. In the bowl of a stand mixer fitted with the paddle attachment, cream the butter and sugar for 5 to 8 minutes on medium speed, or until the mixture is light and pale. With the mixer on low speed, gradually add the flour mixture until it is all incorporated (about 20 seconds) and then slowly add the remaining ½ cup plus 1 tablespoon milk. When all the milk is incorporated, use a rubber spatula to scrape down the bowl. Mix for another 20 seconds on medium speed. Begin adding the egg white mixture in 3 additions, stopping to scrape down the bowl and then mix for another 20 seconds after the last addition. With the mixer on low speed, add the white chocolate in a stream. When it is all incorporated, scrape down the bowl and mix for a final 20 seconds.

6. Divide the batter into the 2 prepared pans; they will be about half full. Using an offset spatula, smooth and level the batter for even baking. Bake for 35 minutes, or until the cakes are golden brown and a skewer inserted into the center comes out clean. Cool the cakes in the pans for 20 minutes. Run a knife around the sides of the pans and invert the cakes onto the prepared rack. Carefully remove the paper and cool completely.

7. Meanwhile, make the whipped cream: In the bowl of a stand mixer fitted with the whisk attachment, whip the heavy cream with the sugar on medium speed until it forms medium-stiff peaks. Transfer the whipped cream into a medium bowl, cover, and refrigerate until ready to use.

8. To make the lemon syrup, whisk together the water and sugar in a small saucepan and simmer for 5 to 8 minutes, or until the liquid has reduced by a third. Remove from the heat, mix in the lemon juice, and set aside.

9. To make the lemon curd, combine the egg yolks, sugar, and lemon juice in a double boiler or a stainless steel bowl set over a small saucepan filled with about 2 inches of water. (The bowl should not touch the water.) Bring the water to a simmer, then whisk the egg mixture slowly but constantly to prevent the yolks from curdling. Cook for 5 to 8 minutes, until the curd has the consistency of jelly. Remove the bowl from the saucepan and whisk in the soft butter 2 tablespoons at a time. When all the butter has been incorporated, push the lemon curd through a fine mesh strainer placed over a medium bowl to remove any lumps. Cover with plastic wrap pressed directly onto the surface of the curd to prevent it from forming a skin. Refrigerate for about 30 minutes to set it up.

10. To make the frosting, melt the white chocolate chips with the canola oil in a double boiler or a stainless steel bowl set over a saucepan, as you did above when making the cake batter. When the chocolate has completely melted, remove the bowl and set aside to cool to room temperature, about 20 minutes.

11. Meanwhile, in the bowl of a stand mixer fitted with the paddle attachment, mix the cream cheese and butter on medium speed for 5 to 8 minutes or until the mixture is light and fluffy. Add the lemon juice and mix briefly, then scrape down the bowl. With the mixer on low speed, pour in the white chocolate and mix for a few minutes, scraping down the bowl as needed to make sure it is fully incorporated. Hold at room temperature until ready to use.

12. To assemble (see Jane's Step-by-Step Tips for Assembling Beautiful Homemade Cakes, page 161), trim the sides, top, and bottom of the cakes with a serrated knife, removing any dark edges and leveling the domed tops. Cut each cake in half horizontally, creating 4 separate layers; choose your best 2 and reserve them for the top and bottom of the cake.

13. Place the bottom layer on a plate or cardboard cake round. Gently brush a third of the lemon syrup onto the layer. Spread evenly with ¼ cup of the raspberry preserves, leaving a 1-inch border around the edge. Pick through the raspberries, reserving 5 beauties for garnish, and place the rest standing up in concentric circles on top of the preserves. Top the berries with the remaining preserves, spreading them as evenly as possible.

14. Add the next cake layer and brush with another third of the lemon syrup. Place 1 cup frosting in the center of the layer and level the frosting, leaving a 1-inch border around the edge. Add the next cake layer and brush with the last third of the lemon syrup. Spread a ⅛-inch layer of whipped cream over the surface, then top with a ⅛-inch layer of lemon curd. Place the final cake layer on top and level the entire cake by gently pressing down on it with the bottom of an empty cake pan. Refrigerate the cake for 20 minutes to set it up.

15. Cover the entire cake with a thin layer of frosting about ⅛ inch thick. This is the crumb coat, so the cake will still be visible through the frosting. Chill the cake for another 20 minutes, holding the remaining frosting at room temperature.

16. For the final coat use a layer of frosting no more than ¼ inch thick. First cover the sides of the cake; the frosting should be evenly

distributed on the offset spatula so that you can coat the sides (top to bottom) all at once. Then frost the top, placing a dollop of frosting in the center and smoothing it out. Finally, square up the top edge. Garnish with the reserved fresh raspberries and sprigs of fresh garden herbs and edible flowers, if desired.

17. For the best presentation, slice the cake using a thin knife: push it slowly through the layers, then wipe the knife clean before making the next cut. Store the frosted cake, well wrapped, in the refrigerator for up to 3 days. Bring it to room temperature (about 2 hours) before serving.

Christmas Cassata Cake

Bûche de Noël, gingerbread spice cake, and persimmon pudding are all traditional holiday table standouts. A specialty each year in the Macrina cafés is this Sicilian cassata cake. Think of a rich orange butter cake filled with a mixture of sweetened ricotta cheese, bittersweet chocolate chunks, candied orange peel, and Cointreau . . . then imagine these lovely flavors all covered in a thin layer of whipped chocolate ganache. Make this cake as soon as you can—no need to wait for a holiday!

MAKES ONE 9-INCH CAKE

1. Position a rack in the center of the oven and preheat to 325°F. Lightly grease two 9-inch round cake pans with canola oil. Cut out two 8-inch parchment paper squares and place them on the bottom of the pans to prevent the cakes from sticking. Line a wire cooling rack with parchment paper. Set aside.

2. To make the batter, sift together the flour, granulated sugar, baking powder, and salt in a medium bowl. Add the orange zest and use your fingertips to mix it in thoroughly, breaking up any moist clumps. Set aside.

3. Combine the egg yolks, vanilla, and ¼ cup of the milk in a medium bowl. Set aside.

4. In the bowl of a stand mixer fitted with the paddle attachment, cream the butter for 5 to 8 minutes, or until it is light, scraping the bowl down occasionally with a rubber spatula to ensure all has been incorporated well. Gradually add the flour mixture until it is incorporated (about 20 seconds), and then slowly add the remaining 1 cup milk. Scrape down the bowl again and mix on medium speed for an additional 30 seconds. With the mixer on low speed, add the egg yolk mixture in 3 additions. Mix for 20 seconds after each addition and scrape down the bowl. The batter should be light-colored and fluffy.

5. Divide the batter evenly between the 2 prepared pans; they will be about two-thirds full. Using an offset spatula, smooth and level the batter for even baking. Bake for 40 to 45 minutes, or until the cakes are deep golden brown and a skewer inserted into the center comes out clean. Cool the cakes in the pans for 20 minutes. Run a knife around the sides of the pans and invert the cakes onto the prepared rack. Carefully

FOR THE BATTER:

2¾ cups cake flour

2¼ cups granulated sugar

1 tablespoon baking powder

½ teaspoon kosher salt

2 tablespoons orange zest (from 2 large oranges)

8 large egg yolks

1 tablespoon pure vanilla extract

¼ cup plus 1 cup whole milk, divided

1 cup (2 sticks) unsalted butter, at room temperature

FOR THE RICOTTA FILLING:

3 ounces good-quality bittersweet chocolate, chopped

22 ounces (3 cups) whole milk ricotta

1 cup confectioners' sugar, sifted

1 tablespoon orange zest

¼ cup diced candied orange peel

1 teaspoon pure vanilla extract

FOR THE COINTREAU SYRUP:

½ cup water

⅓ cup granulated sugar

¼ cup Cointreau or other orange-flavored liqueur

FOR THE GANACHE:

1 cup heavy cream

2 cups (12 ounces) good-quality semisweet chocolate chips

FOR GARNISH:

2 tablespoons diced candied orange peel (optional)

2 fresh holly leaves (optional)

6 pomegranate seeds (optional)

remove the paper and cool completely. (At this point, you can wrap the cakes well and freeze them for up to 2 weeks. Thaw before proceeding.)

6. Meanwhile, to make the filling, mix the chocolate, ricotta, confectioners' sugar, orange zest, candied orange peel, and vanilla in a medium bowl. Set aside.

7. To make the syrup, bring the water and granulated sugar to a simmer over medium heat in a small saucepan. Cook for 3 to 5 minutes, or until the liquid is reduced by a third. Remove the pan from the heat and add the Cointreau. Stir and set aside.

8. To make the ganache, in a small saucepan over medium heat, bring the cream to a froth just before it boils. Turn off the heat and add the chocolate chips, stirring until all the chocolate has melted. Transfer the warm chocolate to a bowl of a stand mixer. Let it cool to room temperature for about 30 minutes, until it is barely warm when you touch the bottom of the bowl, but not yet solidified.

9. To assemble (see Jane's Step-by-Step Tips for Assembling Beautiful Homemade Cakes, page 161), trim the sides, top, and bottom of the cakes with a serrated knife, removing any dark edges and leveling the domed tops. Cut each cake in half horizontally, creating 4 separate layers; choose your best 2 and reserve them for the top and bottom of the cake.

10. Place the bottom layer on a plate or cardboard cake round. Gently brush it with the Cointreau syrup. Place 1 cup of the ricotta filling on the layer and spread it evenly, leaving a 1-inch border around the edge. Repeat this process with the next two layers. Place the final cake layer on top and level the entire cake by gently pressing down on it with the bottom of an empty cake pan. Place the cake in the freezer for 10 to 15 minutes to set up.

11. Meanwhile, place the bowl of ganache on the stand mixer. (If it's too stiff to mix, heat it very briefly over a pan of hot water, stirring until it loosens up.) Using the paddle attachment, mix on low speed for 2 to 3 minutes to aerate the ganache; it will become lighter in color and very spreadable.

12. Remove the cake from the freezer and cover the entire cake with a thin layer of ganache about $\frac{1}{8}$ inch thick. This is the crumb coat, so the

cake will still be visible through the frosting. Chill the cake for another 10 minutes, holding the remaining ganache at room temperature.

13. For the final coat, use a layer of ganache no more than ¼ inch thick. First cover the sides of the cake; the ganache should be evenly distributed on the offset spatula so that you can coat the sides (top to bottom) all at once. Then frost the top, placing a dollop of ganache in the center and smoothing it out. Finally, square up the top edge. Garnish with the candied orange peel placed around the top edge. Place the holly leaves in the center and scatter the pomegranate seeds randomly over the leaves. I always add a light dusting of confectioners' sugar, which creates a nice contrast with the ganache and highlights the garnish.

14. For the best presentation, slice the cake using a thin knife: push it slowly through the layers, then wipe the knife clean before making the next cut. Store the frosted cake, well wrapped, in the refrigerator for up to 4 days. Bring it to room temperature (about 2 hours) before serving.

SAVORY WAYS TO USE OUR BREADS

WITH OUR HECTIC, BUSY LIVES, we often have to think on our toes about preparations for dinner. I may be biased, but I find the answer often lies in basing an impromptu meal around bread and the many roles it can play in a dish. I like to brush sliced bread with olive oil, rub it with fresh garlic, and grill it—perfect for use as croutons with a shellfish and white wine sauté, or topped with a flavorful spread and caramelized cheese. I might thicken a vegetable-rich soup with bread ends for a rustic palate pleaser, or make a salad with seasonal fresh greens and toasted croutons. I always keep pizza crusts in the freezer to top with a few simple ingredients; this satisfies kids and adults alike.

The following recipes all incorporate bread varieties from earlier chapters in this book (I encourage you to improvise, using your favorites). We start with two delicious spreads: first is our Roasted Artichoke Spread with Feta and Oregano, creamy and cheesy, and so tasty with the Fresh Herb Baguette (page 9). Another easy appetizer is the Mission Fig and Kalamata Tapenade served with grilled Hightower Pane Francese bread (page 32) and melted Cambozola cheese.

Using leftover bread, you can craft entrées such as the summery Italian Tomato and Bread Soup, or Macrina's unique version of panzanella (bread salad)—toasted bread cubes tossed with ripe tomatoes, roasted plums, fresh mozzarella, herbs, and arugula. Another favorite is our Best BLT Ever, a twist on the classic, filled with balsamic-roasted nectarines, arugula, bacon, and smoked blue cheese and warmed on a thin loaf of Schiacciatta. Last, there's a recipe for Tarte Flambé (a cousin to those impromptu pizzas mentioned above) topped with *fromage blanc*, smoky bacon, and grilled leeks.

Lunchtime at Macrina is a bustling scene of regulars and local business folks, and these recipes are a sampling of the dishes that we prepare in our café throughout the year. They're designed to be casual, full of bright seasonal flavors, and low stress. The keys to last-minute culinary prowess are having a well-stocked pantry (both sweet and savory), assorted breads in the freezer, and most importantly, a few great recipes to pull off simple, delicious meals with ease and grace.

Roasted Artichoke Spread with Feta and Oregano

1 (14-ounce) can whole artichoke hearts in water, drained and quartered

2 tablespoons pure olive oil

Kosher salt and freshly ground pepper

8 ounces (1 cup) cream cheese, at room temperature

6 ounces (1⅓ cups) crumbled feta cheese, at room temperature

¼ cup extra-virgin olive oil

1 tablespoon plus 1 teaspoon chopped fresh oregano

We've been making artichoke spreads at Macrina for years. They're a great party-crowd pleaser served with crostini, our crisp Sardinian Flatbread with Truffle Salt (page 34), or our focaccia-like Schiacciata (page 27). But don't stop there: try this spread dolloped over sunny-side up eggs, melting slightly and creating a lovely artichoke, oregano, and feta cheese sauce. You could even serve it alongside a grilled chicken breast to enrich and enhance the smoky flavor. There are lots of possibilities!

MAKE 3 CUPS

1. Preheat the oven to 350°F. Line a rimmed baking sheet with parchment paper.

2. In a medium bowl toss the artichokes with the pure olive oil. Spread the artichokes over the prepared baking sheet and season to taste with salt and pepper. Roast for 25 to 30 minutes, or until the artichokes are golden brown on the edges. Cool for 20 minutes.

3. Combine the cream cheese and feta in the bowl of a food processor fitted with the steel blade or a blender. With the machine running, add the extra-virgin olive oil in a slow stream. When the mixture is very smooth, add the oregano and combine for 30 seconds, then add the artichokes and pulse for another minute, or until the artichokes are mostly incorporated but still slightly chunky. Taste and add more salt and pepper, if needed.

4. This spread keeps well for 5 days in the refrigerator. It is best to let it stand at room temperature for about 1 hour before serving, so it will be spreadable.

Mission Fig and Kalamata Tapenade

Macrina hosted a Les Dames d'Escoffier meeting one fall evening to show off our new production facility. The menu included my new favorite tapenade, which features figs and olives—and I was going on to the group about how tasty it was. I had to admit I'd been inspired by a similar spread sold under the Cibo Naturals label. Out of the crowd came Jerilyn Brusseau (who, among many other culinary accomplishments, helped create the Cinnabon roll) saying, "I developed that for Cibo!" Nice to be in such wonderful company! This tapenade is so intensely flavorful that it's best spread thinly and topped with grilled vegetables or cheese. My favorite: spread it on grilled Hightower Pane Francese (page 32) with warmed Cambozola cheese and toasted walnuts. It's also fabulous added to a grilled cheese sandwich or a grilled burger with bacon and gorgonzola.

MAKES 2 CUPS

1 cup dried black mission figs (about 18), trimmed and quartered

1½ cups water

2 tablespoons balsamic vinegar

2 cups pitted kalamata olives, rinsed

1 tablespoon capers

1 tablespoon Dijon-style mustard

2 medium cloves garlic

1½ teaspoons chopped fresh rosemary

1½ teaspoons chopped fresh thyme

½ cup extra-virgin olive oil, divided

1. In a medium saucepan over medium heat, bring the figs, water, and balsamic vinegar to a simmer and cook until the figs are soft and the liquid has reduced to about 2 tablespoons, about 20 minutes. Cool for about 10 minutes.

2. Pour the warm figs and cooking liquid into the bowl of a food processor or a blender. Pulse several times to break down the figs; scrape the bowl and puree to a smooth texture. Add the olives, capers, mustard, garlic, rosemary, thyme, and ¼ cup of the olive oil. Pulse the mixture until it is spreadable and has a uniform texture. With the machine running, add the remaining olive oil in a slow stream until the mixture is perfectly smooth and easy to spread. The tapenade keeps exceptionally well for more than a week in the refrigerator.

Italian Tomato and Bread Soup

8 ripe medium tomatoes (a variety is fine, or go with one type)

¼ cup pure olive oil

3 cloves garlic, crushed and peeled

2½ tablespoons coarsely chopped fresh basil

2 tablespoons coarsely chopped fresh oregano

4 cups (about 6 ounces) day-old white bread, cut into 1-inch cubes

4 cups chicken stock (homemade is best if you have it on hand)

Extra-virgin olive oil, for garnish

Coarse sea salt, for garnish

With the blessings of long, sunny days and warm temperatures throughout the month of August, we Seattle folks really can grow tomatoes! Sweet cherry tomatoes are mostly eaten raw in salads and as off-the-vine snacks, but beefsteaks, romas, and Early Girls are meatier types that make the best soup. Laced with fresh, fragrant basil and oregano, a touch of garlic, chicken stock, and extra-virgin olive oil, this soup is made special by the addition of day-old bread. It thickens the soup and satisfies the soul in a way that only bread can. Our recipe for One-Day Artisan Loaf (page 43) makes an ample loaf, so what you don't eat right away works beautifully in this soup!

MAKES 6 SERVINGS

1. Fill a large saucepan with water and bring it to a boil over high heat. Place a handful of ice cubes in a medium bowl and fill it halfway with cold water: this will be an ice bath to "shock," or stop, the cooking of the tomatoes after they are blanched.

2. Cut a 1-inch X at the base of each tomato, then remove the top core. Gently drop the tomatoes into the boiling water and bring the water back up to a boil. Cook until the skin at the X in the base of the tomatoes peels away easily. This might take only a few seconds or possibly up to a few minutes, depending on the tomatoes' ripeness (the riper they are, the more quickly their skins will loosen). With a slotted spoon, lift the tomatoes out and into the cold-water bath. Cool for 10 minutes.

3. Remove the skins from the tomatoes and discard. Halve the tomatoes and discard the seeds. Coarsely chop the tomatoes into ½-inch pieces and put in a medium bowl. Set aside.

4. Pour the pure olive oil into a medium soup pot over low heat. When the oil is warm, add the crushed garlic. Cook gently for 1 minute (watch so the garlic doesn't burn), then add the basil and oregano and cook, stirring, for another minute. Add the bread cubes and toss so they absorb the oil and herbs. Increase the heat to medium-low and cook for 10 minutes, tossing regularly to lightly brown the bread cubes. Add the tomatoes and increase the heat to medium, releasing their juices. Simmer for 10 minutes.

5. Add the chicken stock and bring the soup back to a simmer, cooking for about 20 minutes to slightly reduce the stock and develop flavor. This is a typical rustic soup, so there is no need to puree, but do use a potato masher or slotted spoon to break up any large chunks. Ladle your bread soup, full of fresh summer flavors, into a shallow soup bowl and top it with a drizzle of extra-virgin olive oil and a sprinkle of coarse sea salt.

Clams with Bacon, Sweet Potatoes, and Garlic-Buttered Crostini

This quick fall supper dish combines the slight saltiness of clams and bacon with the earthy sweetness of the potatoes. The clam liquor, crisp white wine, and cream make a dipping sauce to die for when sopped up with the buttered crostini. For a lighter summer version of this dish, I leave out the cream and swirl in 2 tablespoons of butter to finish the sauce. For great eating and a lovely presentation, serve in large, restaurant-style shallow bowls with rims. That way, all the colors shine through, and you get a little of all the delicious components in every bite. Serve with a simple mixed green salad and a glass of crisp sémillon blanc.

MAKES 4 SERVINGS

1. Place the sweet potatoes in a medium saucepan, cover with water, and add a pinch of salt. Over medium heat simmer the potatoes for 10 minutes or until they are tender when tested with a knife. Drain the potatoes, then transfer to a flat pan or plate to cool.

2. Wash the clams in cold water to remove any sand or grit. If any have opened, discard them, as they are no longer alive. Refrigerate the clams, uncovered, until ready to use.

3. Spread butter onto both sides of the bread slices and place in a large sauté pan over medium heat. Toast the bread on each side, about 3 minutes, until it is golden brown. Remove the bread and rub both sides with the whole garlic clove. Cut each slice on the diagonal and place 2 halves in the bottom of each of four soup bowls, with the bread extending over the sides.

4. Cook the bacon in a large sauté pan over medium-low heat. The bacon should render somewhat slowly, cooking to a golden brown and melting away the fat, about 3 minutes. Add the shallots and cook until translucent, about 2 to 3 minutes. Add the chopped garlic, basil, thyme, and oregano (remember to keep the heat fairly low so that the garlic and herbs cook without burning) and continue cooking for 2 minutes, or until you smell the sweet fragrance of sautéed garlic. Add the clams

1 medium garnet sweet potato (about 10 ounces), peeled and cut into ½-inch dice

3 pounds manila or littleneck clams

¼ cup (½ stick) unsalted butter, at room temperature

4 large slices hearty white, crusty bread (our Pugliese [page 23] or One-Day Artisan Loaf [page 43] works well)

2 cloves garlic, 1 left whole and 1 finely chopped

4 strips thick-cut bacon, cut into ½-inch pieces (Nueske's and Hempler's are great choices)

1 medium shallot, chopped (about ¼ cup)

2 tablespoons coarsely chopped fresh basil

1 tablespoon coarsely chopped fresh thyme

1 teaspoon coarsely chopped fresh oregano

1 cup white wine

1 cup heavy cream

Kosher salt and freshly ground pepper

and white wine. Cover the pan and cook for 5 minutes, or until all the clams have opened. Lift the clams out with a slotted spoon, dividing them among the 4 soup bowls, placing them on the bread. Discard any clams that have not opened.

5. Return the pan to the heat and add the sweet potatoes and cream. Increase the heat a bit and cook for 2 minutes to reheat the potatoes and slightly reduce the cream. Season to taste with salt and pepper. Ladle the potatoes and sauce over the clams.

Macrina's Panzanella

Bread salad is a perfect way to show off delicious artisan bread left over from yesterday's dinner party. Our unique version of panzanella is made with rustic white bread tossed with sweet tomatoes, roasted seasonal fruit, fennel, and arugula. A simple dressing of extra-virgin olive oil and garlic blends with the tomato and fruit juices to make a stunningly fresh-tasting salad. This panzanella often shows up on our café menu served warm with fried eggs for brunch, as a meze (small plate) with a galette slice and soup, or as a fabulous complement to crispy roast chicken.

MAKES 4 TO 6 SERVINGS

1. Position a rack in the center of the oven and preheat to 300°F. Line 3 rimmed baking sheets with parchment paper.

2. Trim the crust from the artisan loaf. Cut enough bread into 1-inch cubes to measure 4 cups. Spread the cubes out on 1 of the prepared baking sheets and toast for 10 to 12 minutes, stirring once or twice until the cubes feel dry on the surface. Set aside to cool.

3. Increase the oven temperature to 350°F.

4. In a medium bowl, toss the plums with 2 tablespoons of the extra-virgin olive oil, then spread on the second prepared baking sheet. Bake the plums for 10 to 15 minutes, or until they are soft. Set aside to cool.

5. Halve the fennel bulb and remove the core by cutting an inverted V at the base. Laying the bulb flat side down, thinly slice the fennel into ¼-inch pieces. Put the fennel in a medium bowl and toss with 2 table-spoons of the extra-virgin olive oil. Spread out on the third prepared baking sheet, season with salt, and roast for 15 minutes, or until the fennel is slightly golden brown on the edges. Set aside to cool.

6. Core the tomatoes and coarsely chop them into ½-inch pieces. (You should have about 3 cups.) Put the tomatoes with all their juices in a large bowl—you'll make the dressing right in the bowl with the tomatoes. Add the garlic, basil, thyme, oregano, salt, and the remaining ¾ cup olive oil. Using a large spoon, toss the ingredients well. Season to taste with pepper. Let the tomatoes macerate (soften and absorb the flavors) for 10 minutes.

½ loaf (about 12 ounces) day-old One-Day Artisan Loaf (page 43)

8 Italian plums, figs, or nectarines, pitted and sliced into ½-inch wedges (about 2 cups), or 2 cups huckleberries

1 cup extra-virgin olive oil, divided

1 medium fennel bulb

3 medium tomatoes

1 medium clove garlic, finely chopped

2 tablespoons coarsely chopped fresh basil

2 teaspoons finely chopped fresh thyme

2 teaspoons finely chopped fresh oregano

½ teaspoon kosher salt

Freshly ground pepper

4 ounces (about 4 medium balls) fresh whole milk mozzarella, cut into ¼-inch slices

3 cups arugula or other flavorful greens (preferably organic)

7. Five minutes before serving, add the bread cubes, plums, fennel, and mozzarella to the bowl with the tomatoes. Toss gently to coat the bread cubes and combine all the ingredients. The bread cubes will absorb the dressing and become tender. When you are ready to serve the salad, toss in the arugula leaves just until they're coated with dressing.

8. The panzanella is best enjoyed the day it's made. If you have a hunch you won't eat it all, prepare the recipe up to the point of macerating the tomatoes and hold back some of the ingredients (untossed) so you can have an encore the next day.

Café Kippered Salmon Salad with Vollkorn Toast

Kippered salmon is a popular find in seafood markets around Seattle and is also generally available in the fresh fish sections of supermarkets around the country. Making kippered salmon is fairly straightforward: first the salmon is rubbed with a salt-and-sugar cure, then slowly hot-smoked to 130°F. Sometimes prior to the smoking, it's basted with a mixture of brown sugar and dark rum—a step that adds another complex dimension of flavor. A true treat! Since both kippered salmon and baby spinach leaves are available year-round, this salad can make its appearance in any season. It's great served as a slightly sophisticated lunch or brunch item.

MAKES 4 SERVINGS

1. Position a rack in the center of the oven and preheat to 325°F.

2. Brush each slice of bread with the olive oil and place on a rimmed baking sheet. Toast the bread for 8 to 10 minutes, or until the slices are slightly brown around the edges. Set aside to cool.

3. Whisk the shallots, orange zest, lemon and orange juice, honey, and dill in a medium bowl and thoroughly combine. Add the sour cream and incorporate fully. Season to taste with salt and pepper. Set the dressing aside.

4. Remove the skin from the salmon and flake the fish into small pieces in a medium bowl. Add the onions, capers, and eggs. Add ¼ cup of the dressing and toss gently to coat.

5. In a separate medium bowl, combine the spinach and endive. Add another ½ cup dressing and toss to evenly coat the greens. Save the extra dressing for another use.

6. To serve, divide the greens among 4 plates. Place a quarter of the salmon mixture on the tossed greens and tuck two slices of toast slightly into the salmon mixture, extending beyond the plate's edge. Season to taste with salt and pepper.

1 loaf Vollkorn Bread (page 5) or other dense, German-style whole grain bread, cut into ¼-inch slices

2 tablespoons pure olive oil

2 tablespoons finely chopped shallots

1 teaspoon orange zest

¼ cup freshly squeezed lemon juice (from about 1 large lemon)

1 tablespoon freshly squeezed orange juice

1 tablespoon honey

2 teaspoons fresh chopped dill or basil

½ cup low-fat sour cream

Kosher salt and freshly ground pepper

6 ounces kippered (hot-smoked) salmon

½ small red onion, thinly sliced

2 tablespoons capers

4 hard-cooked eggs, quartered

4 cups baby spinach leaves

2 spears endive, thinly sliced

✻ LOOK AT THOSE SANDWICHES! ✻

Creating a truly perfect sandwich can take months of grueling research and development! Every detail is important: the secret marinade, the even-more-secret sauce, the best technique to keep the filling moist, deciding whether a layer of grilled veggies or cheese would be a plus, lettuce or no lettuce. The bread selection is crucial too. It needs to confidently hold the sandwich "inners" without becoming too large to get your mouth around. It must also have a crust strong enough to hold in the juices—but not be so crusty that all the ingredients cascade into your lap when you bite down.

Lucky for us, there's a small, funky Caribbean restaurant here in Seattle called Paseo. It actually has two locations, both reminiscent of those picturesque boardwalk sandwich huts on your favorite tropical beach. Paseo has done its homework and crafts many amazing, award-winning sandwiches. But they all have one very important thing in common: every last one is built upon a Macrina Bakery Giuseppe roll: a stubby baguette-type bread with a thin, crisp crust and a fragrant, flavorful interior!

Their signature sandwich is the Cuban Roast, made with heaps of succulent pulled pork that's marinated with Lorenzo Lorenzo's (owner and chef-originator) own secret spice combination. Into the Giuseppe roll goes a generous slather of seasoned aioli, fresh cilantro, crisp romaine, insanely good thick-cut, char-grilled onion rings, pickled jalapeños, and that flavorful, juicy pork! It's all securely wrapped in sandwich paper to keep the juices intact, and the paper doubles as a plate—since you can't possibly wait to get home to eat. In fact, if you've come to their waterfront location, you might as well sit down at a picnic table right outside the pink shack and have at it.

These sandwiches have an incredible following—to the tune of 1,500 to 1,800 of our Giuseppe rolls a day. This requires that four of Macrina's busy bakers work for two to three hours daily to form and shape these signature rolls. The baking process takes about four hours to complete—then, after the rolls cool, the drivers gingerly pack them up and whisk them off for delivery before the restaurants open at 11 a.m. to lines of hungry fans. Paseo is the largest one-product customer we have, and we're thrilled to be part of their success. March on, Lorenzo!

Pastrami, Caramelized Onion, and Gruyère Sandwich

Onion rye, sliced sourdough, or challah would all be great breads for this sandwich. At Macrina, we often feature it on our Pretzel Knot Roll, a fairly dense roll made with the addition of a little rye flour, then topped with coarse salt, poppy seeds, and sesame seeds. The combination of these flavors with the American favorite delicacy of thinly sliced peppery pastrami, plus sweet caramelized onions and nutty gruyère cheese, is terrific.

MAKES 4 SANDWICHES

1. To make the caramelized onions, melt the butter in a large nonstick sauté pan over medium-low heat. Add the onions and toss to coat. Cook until the onions have softened, about 5 minutes, and add the thyme and red pepper flakes. Continue caramelizing the onions, stirring them frequently so they brown evenly, for 20 to 25 minutes. (If the heat is too hot, the onions will burn—so take some time to enjoy the process.) Season to taste with salt. Transfer the onions to a large bowl and set aside.

2. To make the mustard aioli, whisk the egg yolk, garlic, lemon juice, and mustard in a medium bowl to thoroughly combine. Start adding the canola oil just a few drops at a time, whisking constantly, until the mixture begins to emulsify. As it thickens, continue adding the oil in a slow stream, making sure each addition is thoroughly blended before adding more. Season to taste with salt, then cover the aioli and refrigerate until needed.

3. Position a rack in the center of the oven and preheat to 350°F. Line a rimmed baking sheet with parchment paper and set aside.

4. Cut the pretzel rolls in half horizontally. Spread the butter equally on the rolls and place them cut side down on the prepared baking sheet. Toast the rolls in the oven for 3 to 5 minutes, or until the butter is melted and the rolls are warm.

5. To assemble the sandwiches, flip each roll over so that the cut side is up. Spread each side with some mustard aioli. Place equal amounts of pastrami on the bottom halves of the rolls, folding it up to only slightly overhang. Next, divide the caramelized onions and layer them on top

FOR THE CARAMELIZED ONIONS:

¼ cup (½ stick) unsalted butter, cut into large pieces

2 medium yellow or Walla Walla onions, cut into ⅛-inch slices

1 teaspoon chopped fresh thyme

¼ teaspoon crushed red pepper flakes

Kosher salt

FOR THE MUSTARD AIOLI:

1 large egg yolk

½ teaspoon finely chopped garlic

1½ teaspoons freshly squeezed lemon juice

1 tablespoon plus 1 teaspoon Dijon-style mustard

½ cup canola oil

FOR THE SANDWICHES:

4 Pretzel Knot Rolls (page 14)

2 tablespoons unsalted butter

10 to 12 thin slices (about 14 ounces) good-quality pepper-crusted pastrami

4 ounces gruyère cheese, thinly sliced

of the pastrami. Place the gruyère slices on the top halves of the rolls. Return the sandwiches, still open faced, to the oven for 5 minutes, or until the cheese is melted and the pastrami is warm to the touch.

6. Put the sandwiches together and cut on the diagonal with a serrated knife.

Vietnamese Crab Sandwich with Ginger Aioli and Veggie Slaw

A treasured delicacy in the Pacific Northwest is fresh, beautiful Dungeness crab. They're almost always available in our markets since they're shipped in year-round from Alaska, as well as harvested seasonally from our cold Puget Sound waters. Here, the sweet, slightly salty, tender flesh is simply tossed with lemon juice and sesame oil to allow the crab flavors to shine. Then to accent those flavors, we add a zippy ginger aioli and crisp fresh vegetable slaw—typical of a Vietnamese bahn mi *sandwich—creating a combination that's bright, colorful, and delicious.*

NOTE: This sandwich also works great as a "slider." Simply halve the size of the roll dough balls (you'll get twenty-four 1½-ounce rolls) and bake for 10 to 12 minutes.

MAKES 4 SANDWICHES

1. To make the vegetable slaw, toss the carrots, daikon, green onions, rice wine vinegar, sugar, and salt in a medium bowl. Set aside.

2. To make the ginger aioli, whisk the egg yolks, mustard, garlic, ginger, and lemon juice in a medium bowl to thoroughly combine. Start adding the canola oil just a few drops at a time, whisking constantly, until the mixture begins to emulsify. As it thickens, continue adding the oil in a slow stream, making sure each addition is thoroughly blended before adding more. The finished aioli will be slightly thick but won't look like traditional store-bought mayonnaise. Season with the salt and cayenne.

3. To assemble the sandwiches, gently toss the crabmeat, lemon juice, sesame oil, cilantro, green onions, and red pepper flakes in a medium bowl to combine—you may need to add a pinch of salt to bring the flavors together. Cut the rolls in half horizontally and spread each half equally with the butter. Brown the buttered side of the rolls in a large sauté pan (or under the broiler). Place the toasted rolls face up on 4 plates. Spread each bottom bun with equal amounts of the ginger aioli, then layer on the vegetable slaw and finish with the seasoned crabmeat. Top each sandwich with the remaining bun and cut in half with a serrated knife. Toothpicks may be necessary to hold the sandwiches together.

FOR THE VEGETABLE SLAW:

2 medium carrots, grated (about 1 cup)

½ medium daikon radish, grated (about 1 cup)

2 green onions, thinly sliced

3 tablespoons unseasoned rice wine vinegar

1 tablespoon sugar

1 teaspoon kosher salt

FOR THE GINGER AIOLI:

2 large egg yolks

1 teaspoon Dijon-style mustard

½ teaspoon chopped garlic

1 tablespoon plus 1½ teaspoons minced fresh ginger

2 tablespoons freshly squeezed lemon juice

1 cup canola oil

½ teaspoon kosher salt

⅛ teaspoon cayenne

FOR THE SANDWICHES:

8 ounces fresh Dungeness crabmeat, picked over

1 tablespoon freshly squeezed lemon juice

1 teaspoon sesame oil

¼ cup chopped fresh cilantro

2 green onions, thinly sliced

⅛ teaspoon crushed red pepper flakes

4 SoDo Rolls (page 12), or other sandwich-size rolls

2 tablespoons unsalted butter

Best BLT Ever

2 medium nectarines, cut into
½-inch wedges

1 tablespoon balsamic vinegar

1 tablespoon extra-virgin olive oil

2 tablespoons coarsely chopped
fresh basil

12 strips thick-cut bacon (I prefer
Nueske's or Hempler's)

2 loaves Schiacciata (page 27)

½ cup mayonnaise

2 medium beefsteak tomatoes,
cored and sliced about ¼ inch
thick

20 large arugula leaves

4 ounces smoke-flavored blue
cheese (I prefer Salemville
Smokehaus Blue)

Being a big fan of bacon, I thought it was natural to feature an updated BLT in this book. This version is inspired by the colors and flavors of summer: it features balsamic-roasted nectarines tossed with fresh basil, thick-cut bacon, thin-cut tomatoes, arugula, and smoky blue cheese. Truly, your imagination can go wild creating spectacular combinations with almost any kind of cured meat, greens, and tomatoes. (And I can't resist adding cheese.) Any soft-crusted, flat bread such as focaccia or Hightower Pane Francese (page 32) makes a great BLT, but our Schiacciata bread makes the best backdrop because of its lovely olive oil and fresh herb flavors and its thin profile (you won't fill up on bread!).

MAKES 4 SANDWICHES

1. Position a rack in the center of the oven and preheat to 375°F. Line a rimmed baking sheet with parchment paper.

2. Toss the nectarines with the balsamic vinegar and olive oil in a medium bowl. Transfer to the prepared baking sheet, spreading the nectarines in a single layer for even roasting. Roast for 25 minutes, or until the nectarines are lightly browned and soft. Transfer to a medium bowl to cool. When they are room temperature, toss with the basil. Set aside.

3. In a large sauté pan over medium-low heat, cook the bacon strips for about 8 minutes, turning them over frequently with tongs so that the fat renders evenly and the bacon becomes deep golden brown. (This will most likely need to be done in two batches. Pour off any excess fat between batches.) Remove from the pan to a paper towel–lined plate and set aside.

4. Lower the oven temperature to 325°F.

5. Cut each Schiacciata loaf into two 6-inch-long pieces, using a serrated knife. Then cut each piece horizontally, creating the tops and bottoms for the sandwiches. Place the bread on a rimmed baking sheet and warm in the oven for 3 to 5 minutes.

6. To assemble the sandwiches, spread the bottoms of the bread with a thin layer of mayonnaise. Begin layering your ingredients on top, starting with the reserved nectarines; then pile on the tomatoes, reserved bacon, and arugula. Crumble a little blue cheese on the top side of the bread and spread it thinly with a spatula to cover the whole piece. Put the sandwiches together and cut on the diagonal with a serrated knife.

Tarte Flambé with Bacon and Fromage Blanc

8 strips thick-cut bacon

2 medium sweet onions, cut into ¼-inch rings

2 tablespoons chopped fresh thyme, divided

2 tablespoons extra-virgin olive oil

Kosher salt and freshly ground pepper

1 pound Mt. Townsend Creamery fromage blanc or other mild spreadable goat cheese

1 recipe Grilled Pizza Crusts (page 49)

¼ cup heavy cream

About ¼ cup cornmeal, for sprinkling

What is tarte flambé? Something prepared tableside, cooked with alcohol, and set afire? Guess again: It got its name from taking a flattened piece of bread dough and baking it on the floor of a wood-burning oven. This typical Alsatian tart is topped with bacon lardons, and the drippings, or "spits," of fat create flames—thus, the name "flambé." These few simple ingredients combine brilliantly for a tasty appetizer or entrée accompanied by a salad. The cured bacon imparts a smoky flavor, and is heavenly paired with the fromage blanc *and thinly sliced onions. Our Grilled Pizza Crusts work exceptionally for this recipe. Piadina bread (page 25) would also work well.*

MAKES FOUR 8-INCH TARTS

1. In a large sauté pan over medium heat, slowly cook the bacon strips (fitting as many as possible side by side) for about 5 minutes, turning them over frequently with tongs so that the fat renders evenly and the bacon starts to color but doesn't get crisp. (This will most likely need to be done in two batches. Pour off any excess fat between batches.) Remove from the pan to a paper towel–lined plate and cool for 10 minutes. Cut the bacon strips into ½-inch pieces and set aside.

2. Place a baking stone on the center rack of the oven and preheat to 400°F. Line a rimmed baking sheet with parchment paper and set aside.

3. Toss the onions in a medium bowl with 1 tablespoon of the thyme and the olive oil. Place the onions on the prepared baking sheet and season to taste with salt and pepper. Place the baking sheet on the baking stone and cook for 5 to 8 minutes, or until the onions are translucent and just darkening on the edges. Cool for 10 minutes.

4. Crumble the fromage blanc evenly onto the pizza crusts. Top each crust with the reserved bacon and roasted onions, scattering them to make a pretty design. Sprinkle with the cream, remaining 1 tablespoon thyme, and salt and pepper to taste.

5. Sprinkle a baker's peel with cornmeal, lift the pizzas onto the peel, and slide them onto the baking stone. Bake for 5 to 8 minutes, or until the crust is deep golden brown, the cheese is melted, and the bacon crispy. Cool for a few minutes before serving.

BRUNCH FAVORITES

OUR ORIGINAL CAFÉ in Seattle's Belltown neighborhood—all 25 seats' worth—is a bevy of brunch madness. We serve more than 125 hungry guests in that crowded space each weekend day from a kitchen that's compact, to say the least. With only four electric burners, a soup warmer, and our trusty Bakers Pride pizza oven, we've learned to make dishes that are simple to prepare but big on flavor. Brunch starts at 9 a.m., but customers seat themselves way before that in anticipation of the breakfast soon to be delivered to their tables. Just imagine: steaming-hot espresso drinks arrive tableside, followed by a colorful cup of fresh fruit. Maybe you've ordered our weekend special of thick-cut brioche French toast with brown sugar–roasted peaches and cream, or a slice of the seasonal quiche. However you choose to indulge, the atmosphere is warm and friendly, and it's a great way to begin a weekend morning!

Favorite Macrina brunch dishes fill this chapter. Look for the Fresh Herb Scramble with Humboldt Fog Goat Cheese and Cherry Tomatoes, or the velvety Orange Brioche French Toast with Raspberries and Amaretto Whipped Cream. For a heartier option, our Breakfast Hash, made with loads of fresh roasted vegetables, is topped with fried eggs and shaved manchego cheese. And you can never go wrong with Elizabeth's Biscuits with Roasted Fennel–Sausage Gravy; it's crazy good, with Italian chicken sausage and hints of mustard and cayenne—all in a creamy sauce over eggs and warm biscuits.

As you think about the flavors in these brunch entrées, consider complementing them with a fresh-baked pastry or some slices of toasted artisan bread. Recipes from the previous chapters—including the Fresh Herb Baguette (page 9), One-Day Artisan Whole Grain Bread (page 46), or just about any recipe from the Muffins, Scones, and Coffee Cakes chapter (page 73)—would be outstanding.

Bring a little Macrina to your weekend and celebrate Sundays as they were intended. Enjoy a newspaper, endless cups of fresh-brewed coffee, and warm delectables—from our humble kitchen to yours!

Breakfast Rice Pudding with Honeyed Yogurt, Seasonal Fruit, and Almonds

1 cup plain nonfat yogurt

2 tablespoons local honey

2 cups ripe seasonal fruit

1 cup basmati rice

3 cups water

Pinch of kosher salt

1½ cups whole milk

⅓ cup sugar

2 teaspoons pure vanilla extract

½ cup sliced almonds, toasted
(see Toasting Tips, page 7)

Hot breakfast cereals are a quick, nutritious, and flavorful way to start your day. This is a simple breakfast version of rice pudding that's not overly heavy with cream or strong spice flavors. I love the refreshing sweetened yogurt, seasonal fruit, and crunchy toasted nuts. Nice alternatives to the basmati rice in this recipe are oatmeal, quinoa, multigrain whole cereal or, of course, brown rice. The cooking times will vary, so prepare according to package instructions.

MAKES 4 SERVINGS

1. Whisk the yogurt and honey in a small bowl and set aside.

2. Wash, pare, pit, cut, dice, or otherwise prepare your fruit(s) of choice so that they are bite-size. Set aside.

3. Put the rice in a medium saucepan. Run cold water into the pan and swirl the rice around, releasing some of its starch (the water will look cloudy). Pour off the water and repeat. Drain the rice, then add the 3 cups water and a pinch or two of salt. Cover the pot with the lid slightly ajar and place the pan over medium heat to cook. The rice will begin to simmer; lower the heat to maintain a simmer and cook for 10 minutes, or until most the water has been absorbed. Add the milk, sugar, and vanilla. Replace the lid slightly ajar and keep the heat low for the final 6 minutes of cooking. Check the rice for tenderness. There should still be ample milk in the pan to serve in each bowl—enough to pool at the edges. If the rice has absorbed all the milk, add a little extra.

4. To serve, top each bowl of pudding with a generous dollop of honeyed yogurt, then add some of the almonds and fruit.

5. I will save uneaten rice pudding for several days, to enjoy later in the week. Simply add more milk to cover, reheat in a saucepan or in the microwave, and top with your garnish of choice.

Elizabeth's Biscuits with Roasted Fennel–Sausage Gravy

I'm a certified member of the Breakfast Biscuits and Gravy Club. If it is listed on a brunch menu (and the gravy is homemade), then heaven help me—I'm ordering it! Elizabeth Hall, our head chef for savory foods at Macrina, makes a mean gravy and biscuits. She usually uses Italian chicken sausage but has also used juniper and garlic pork sausage from Seattle's wonderful Link Lab Artisan Meats. Both are over-the-top good! Have fun with this recipe—you too will get hooked.

MAKES 4 SERVINGS

1. To make the biscuits, position a rack in the center of the oven and preheat to 375°F. Line 2 rimmed baking sheets with parchment paper and set aside.

2. Sift together the flours, baking powder, and salt in a medium bowl. Make a well in the center of the flour and pour in 1½ cups of the cream. Using a rubber spatula, begin pulling the flour into the cream; mix just enough to combine the dough into a shaggy mass. (As with any biscuit dough, do not overwork this—you'll end up with tough biscuits.) When almost all the flour is incorporated, transfer the dough from the bowl onto a floured work surface and pat it into a 4-by-8-inch rectangle. I usually cut the dough into 8 equal squares, but you can also use a flour-dipped glass or biscuit cutter and punch out 8 rounds.

3. Place the biscuits on one of the prepared baking sheets, spacing them 2 inches apart. Brush the tops of the biscuits with the remaining 2 tablespoons of cream. Bake for 20 to 25 minutes, or until the biscuits are light golden brown on the edges and bottom. Cool on the sheet for 20 minutes, then transfer to a wire rack to cool completely.

4. To make the gravy, trim, halve, and core the fennel bulb. Chop enough fronds to measure 2 teaspoons and set aside. Placing the halves cut side down on a cutting board, slice them vertically, then slice in the opposite direction, creating ½-inch dice.

5. Toss the diced fennel with the olive oil, season to taste with salt and pepper, and transfer to the other prepared baking sheet, spreading the pieces so they roast evenly. Bake for 15 minutes, or until the fennel is golden brown on the edges. Set aside to cool.

FOR THE BISCUITS:

1 cup unbleached all-purpose flour

1 cup cake flour

2 teaspoons baking powder

1¼ teaspoons kosher salt

1½ cups plus 2 tablespoons heavy cream, divided

FOR THE GRAVY:

1 medium fennel bulb with fronds

1 tablespoon pure olive oil

Kosher salt and freshly ground pepper

1 tablespoon canola oil

8 ounces (1 cup) bulk Italian chicken sausage (I prefer Isernio's)

3 tablespoons unsalted butter

½ teaspoon whole fennel seeds, finely ground

¼ teaspoon dry mustard powder

¼ teaspoon freshly grated nutmeg

¼ teaspoon cayenne

3 tablespoons unbleached all-purpose flour

2 cups whole milk

1½ cups heavy cream

FOR THE EGGS:

2 tablespoons unsalted butter

Kosher salt and freshly ground pepper

8 large eggs

2 teaspoons chopped fresh Italian parsley

6. Place a large sauté pan over medium heat. Add the canola oil, coating the bottom of the pan. After about 1 minute (the pan should be quite hot), add the sausage. Using a wooden spoon, break the sausage into small pieces, tossing to cook thoroughly. When the sausage is completely cooked, about 4 minutes, pour it into a strainer fitted over a medium bowl to catch the rendered fat. (Often with chicken sausage there is little or no excess fat, but with pork varieties you may see more. You can substitute the rendered sausage fat for the butter called for in this recipe, if you like.) Set aside.

7. Return the sauté pan to the burner, again over medium heat. Add the butter and melt completely. Add the fennel seed, mustard, nutmeg, ½ teaspoon salt, and cayenne. Sprinkle in the flour and, using a whisk, combine the dry ingredients with the fat to create a roux (cooked flour and fat that will thicken the gravy). Cook for 1 to 2 minutes, whisking, until the roux is a deep gold color. Reduce the heat to low and add the milk in a slow stream. Whisk the milk into the roux as you go, combining it completely (almost making a paste) before adding more milk—if you add the milk too quickly, you'll end up with those dreaded lumps! Add the heavy cream and reserved fennel and sausage. Cook for 20 to 25 minutes—you want to cook out the raw flour taste and allow the gravy to thicken. Check the seasoning, adding additional salt and pepper to taste. Keep the gravy warm on the stovetop.

8. Preheat the oven to 275°F. Line your counter with 4 plates. Cut the biscuits in half horizontally and place 2 biscuits in the center of each plate. Lift off the biscuit tops and set on the rim of the plate.

9. To make the eggs, melt ½ tablespoon of the butter in a small non-stick pan over medium heat, swirling to coat the bottom of the pan. When the butter is sizzling, crack 2 eggs into the pan. Sprinkle with a little salt and pepper. Flip the eggs after the whites have congealed, about 1 minute. Cook to your desired firmness. Place the hot eggs onto a biscuit, transfer the plate to the warm oven, and repeat with the remaining butter and eggs. (As an alternative, make scrambled eggs—they go very quickly and you can cook all the eggs at the same time.)

10. To serve, ladle about ¾ cup of warm gravy over each plate of eggs, place the biscuit tops on at an angle (so the eggs and gravy show a bit),

and sprinkle with the parsley and reserved fennel fronds. Are you hungry yet?

11. If you don't use all the biscuits and gravy, they freeze well (keep them separate) for up to 2 weeks. When reheating the gravy, it may need to be re-emulsified: warm it in a saucepan over medium heat with a bit more cream or milk, stirring until smooth.

Fresh Herb Scramble with Humboldt Fog Goat Cheese and Cherry Tomatoes

2 cups cherry tomatoes, stemmed and halved

1 tablespoon plus 1 teaspoon extra-virgin olive oil

Kosher salt

4 ounces Humboldt Fog goat cheese or other dry-aged goat cheese

8 large eggs

1 tablespoon chopped fresh chervil

1 tablespoon snipped fresh chives

1 tablespoon chopped fresh Italian parsley

3 tablespoons extra-virgin olive oil

Working with a few simple ingredients and handling them with great integrity creates some of the best dishes ever. Finding those ingredients is easily accomplished when you shop at your local farmers' market. You should be able to buy fresh eggs with bright-orange yolks; sweet, true-tasting tomatoes; and many unique regional artisan products such as cheeses, dried meats, and specialty wines. In the height of the tomato season, this dish is one of Macrina's best sellers. It is delicious served with buttered toast made from our seeded baguette loaf.

MAKES 4 SERVINGS

1. Toss the cherry tomatoes gently with the olive oil and a pinch of kosher salt in a medium bowl. Set aside.

2. Cut the goat cheese vertically, starting at the tip of the wedge and moving toward the wider back. This delicious cheese naturally falls apart at the center ash line—let it crumble as it will. Set aside.

3. Crack the eggs into a medium bowl and add the chervil, chives, and parsley. Whisk to thoroughly combine.

4. In a large sauté pan over medium heat, add the olive oil. When it is warm, about 1 minute, add the eggs (you want them to begin setting up when they hit the pan, but not to turn brown). Using a rubber spatula, gently move the cooked edges aside, allowing the liquid eggs to run to the bare surfaces of the pan and cook. When the eggs are cooked to your liking, season to taste with salt.

5. To serve, divide the eggs among 4 plates. Top each plate with one-quarter of the seasoned tomatoes and one-quarter of the crumbled cheese.

Macrina's Breakfast Hash

We always feature a weekly market special at brunch: "This Week's Hot Picks" are selected from the most recently harvested crops brought in by local farmers. Many different roasted vegetable combinations have made their way onto the menu, but this is a big favorite: it's a hearty breakfast hash made of roasted brussels sprouts, Yukon Gold potatoes, sweet caramelized onions, garlic, pancetta, and shaved manchego cheese. All you need to add is a cup of strong, dark-roast, Seattle-style coffee.

MAKES 4 SERVINGS

1. Position a rack in the center of the oven and preheat to 350°F. Line 2 rimmed baking sheets with parchment paper. Set aside.

2. Place the brussels sprouts and onions in a medium bowl and toss with 2 tablespoons of the olive oil. Transfer to one of the prepared baking sheets and season to taste with salt. Bake for 20 to 25 minutes, or until the vegetables are golden brown on the edges. Set aside.

3. Toss the potatoes in a medium bowl with the remaining 2 tablespoons olive oil. Transfer the potatoes to the other lined baking sheet and season to taste with salt. Bake for 30 to 35 minutes, or until the potatoes are tender and golden brown.

4. In a large sauté pan over medium-low heat, sauté the pancetta slowly, stirring occasionally. When the pieces are curled on the edges and golden brown, add the garlic and cook for 1 minute, just to heat it through but not brown. Add the brussels sprouts, onions, and potatoes and gently toss. Keep warm while you prepare the eggs.

5. Place a large nonstick sauté pan over medium heat. Melt the butter, swirling to coat the bottom of the pan. When the butter is sizzling, crack the eggs into the pan. Season to taste with salt and pepper. When the egg whites have congealed, flip the eggs over and cook for another few minutes to set the yolks to your liking.

6. To serve, divide the warm hash among 4 plates, placing it in the center. Lay 2 cooked eggs over the hash. Shave the manchego over the top with a vegetable peeler. (If you shave the cheese in advance, it is best to keep it covered with plastic wrap and chilled.)

8 medium brussels sprouts (about 5 ounces), trimmed and cut into ¼-inch ribbons

1 medium yellow onion, cut into ¼-inch slices

4 tablespoons pure olive oil, divided

Kosher salt

3 medium Yukon Gold potatoes, cut into ½-inch dice

6 thin slices pancetta (about 3 ounces), cut into ½-inch pieces

2 teaspoons finely chopped garlic

2 tablespoons unsalted butter

8 large eggs

Freshly ground pepper

2 ounces manchego cheese

Savory Bread Pudding with Roasted Leeks, Cremini Mushrooms, and Gruyère

½ loaf day-old hearty white bread, crusts removed, cut into ¾-inch cubes (about 4 cups)

2 medium leeks

4 tablespoons pure olive oil, divided

8 medium cremini mushrooms, cut into ¼-inch slices

1 cup whole milk

1 cup half-and-half

2 tablespoons chopped fresh Italian parsley

2 large eggs

2 large egg yolks

½ teaspoon kosher salt

¼ cup (½ stick) unsalted butter, melted

5 ounces gruyère cheese, grated (about 2 cups)

Bread puddings are a comfort food that most often play the role of a sweet item for breakfast or dessert. This recipe is a savory version with the wonderful qualities of velvety, custard-soaked bread; a cheesy, caramelized crust; and the added depth of roasted vegetables. Each season holds its bounty of fresh ingredients, so use your imagination and improvise! Always popular is a brunch version using bacon or ham, along with your choice of cheese. This savory pudding can be assembled the night before (to the point of covering it with aluminum foil) and then baked the next day. If you'll be baking it right from the fridge, allow a bit of extra oven time.

MAKES 6 TO 8 SERVINGS

1. Position a rack in the center of the oven and preheat to 300°F. Line 2 rimmed baking sheets with parchment paper and grease a 9-inch pie plate with canola oil. Set aside.

2. Scatter the bread cubes on one of the baking sheets and toast in the oven for 10 to 12 minutes, or until they are dry and just lightly colored on the edges. Set aside to cool.

3. Trim the leeks an inch above the white part (extending into the light-green area) and at the root. Slice them in half lengthwise and wash out any excess sand you find. Place them cut side down and slice them into ¼-inch pieces.

4. Heat 2 tablespoons of the olive oil in large nonstick sauté pan over medium heat, swirling to coat the bottom of the pan. When the oil is hot, add the leeks and sauté until they are translucent and slightly golden brown, about 5 minutes. Transfer to a medium bowl to cool.

5. Add the remaining 2 tablespoons of olive oil to the pan. When the oil is hot, add the mushrooms and cook for 5 to 8 minutes, tossing them occasionally. (When they first start to wilt, the mushrooms will exude moisture. Just continue cooking them; the liquid will cook off.) When the mushrooms are a deep golden brown, transfer them to a bowl to cool.

6. Whisk the milk, half-and-half, parsley, eggs, egg yolks, and salt in a medium bowl. Set the custard aside.

7. Increase the oven temperature to 325°F.

8. Place the bread cubes in a large bowl. Toss with the melted butter, coating well. Add the reserved leeks and mushrooms, and the gruyère. Toss to distribute evenly. Transfer the mixture to the prepared baking dish, spreading it out evenly—it's important to not pack in the bread. It will stand taller than the dish by maybe ½ inch. Pour the custard over the bread mixture, working your way around the dish to allow the bread to soak up a consistent amount of custard. Cover with aluminum foil and let sit for 30 minutes at room temperature so the bread can soak up the custard.

9. Place the baking dish on the second prepared baking sheet and bake for 1 hour and 10 minutes. Press down lightly in the center to see if the custard is set or still liquid. If still liquid, bake it, covered, for a few more minutes. When it is set, remove the foil and return the pudding to the oven for another 20 minutes to crisp and caramelize the bread and cheese on top.

10. Cool the pudding in the pan for 30 minutes before serving. It will keep for 3 days well wrapped in the refrigerator.

Orange Brioche French Toast with Raspberries and Amaretto Whipped Cream

We always offer a french toast item on our brunch menu. Each week's variation is slightly different, featuring one of our many freshly baked brioches (such as sour cherry, chocolate with orange, or raisin), seasonal and local fruits, and a complementing whipped cream. This recipe is built around our candied orange brioche; you can also use a loaf of basic brioche or rich egg bread—just add 2 teaspoons of fresh orange zest to the custard and you're good to go.

MAKES 4 SERVINGS

1. Position a rack in the center of the oven and preheat to 300°F.

2. Crack the eggs into a medium bowl, then add the orange juice, ½ cup of the cream, vanilla, cinnamon, nutmeg, and brown sugar. Use a whisk to combine the custard mixture well.

3. In a separate medium bowl, combine the remaining 1 cup cream with the granulated sugar and amaretto. Using a clean whisk or an electric mixer, whip the cream until it forms medium peaks. Cover and refrigerate until needed.

4. Dip the brioche slices into the custard mixture, coating both sides. Place on a rimmed baking sheet to rest, turning once or twice so that the custard soaks in evenly.

5. Place a large sauté pan or pancake griddle over medium heat and add about 1 tablespoon of the butter. Once it is sizzling nicely (not smoking), add as many brioche slices as will fit. Cook for about 2 minutes on the first side; flip when the slices are a deep golden brown. As the pieces cook, transfer them to another baking sheet and place the pan in the oven to keep warm. (This also gives the french toast a second opportunity to cook all the way through and get a little crispy.) Repeat with the remaining butter and brioche.

5 large eggs

¼ cup freshly squeezed orange juice

1½ cups heavy cream, divided

1½ teaspoons pure vanilla extract

¼ teaspoon ground cinnamon

¼ teaspoon freshly grated nutmeg

2 tablespoons light brown sugar

3 tablespoons granulated sugar

2 tablespoons amaretto or other almond-flavored liqueur

1 loaf Candied Orange Brioche or other egg bread, cut into eight 1-inch slices

¼ cup (½ stick) unsalted butter

2 cups (1 pint) fresh raspberries

Confectioners' sugar, for garnish

6. Cut each slice of french toast on the diagonal and arrange 4 halves in the center of each plate, setting them at perpendicular angles. Divide the raspberries among the four plates, scattering them randomly over the top of the toast. Finish with a generous dollop of amaretto whipped cream and a sprinkle of confectioners' sugar. Warm maple syrup is definitely welcome also!

Pecan Waffles with Maple-Roasted Bananas and Vanilla Whipped Cream

Seattle is a big breakfast town, and waffles seem to be everyone's favorite weekend indulgence. I think it has something to do with our weather—the comfort of a warm, sweet breakfast brightens the day ahead. This old-fashioned buttermilk waffle is dressed up with toasted pecans, brown sugar, maple syrup, and cinnamon-roasted bananas, and then topped with lightly sweetened vanilla whipped cream. To complete the meal, serve with breakfast sausage links or crisp bacon. Seven a.m. never looked so good.

MAKES 4 SERVINGS

1. Position a rack in the center of the oven and preheat to 325°F. Line a rimmed baking sheet with parchment paper and set it aside.

2. To make the waffles, in a medium bowl, sift the flours, baking soda, ⅓ cup of the granulated sugar, and salt. Add the pecans and combine well. Set aside.

3. Whisk the egg yolks, buttermilk, and melted butter in a medium bowl. Using either an electric mixer or a whisk, whip the whites until they form medium-stiff peaks.

4. Drizzle the yolk mixture into the flour mixture and whisk to combine, making sure any lumps are dissolved. Using a rubber spatula, gently fold in the whites. Take care to not overmix and deflate the batter. (It will hold in the refrigerator for 2 to 3 hours.)

5. To make the roasted bananas, toss the bananas with the maple syrup, brown sugar, and cinnamon in a medium bowl. Transfer to the prepared baking sheet and dot with the butter. Bake for 10 minutes, or until the bananas are slightly golden brown and soft. Transfer to a bowl to cool. Set aside.

6. To make the vanilla whipped cream, in the bowl of a stand mixer fitted with the whisk attachment, whip the heavy cream, vanilla, and the remaining 3 tablespoons granulated sugar until they form medium-stiff peaks. (Or whip by hand with a whisk; it will help if the bowl, whisk, and cream are all cold.) Refrigerate until ready to use.

FOR THE WAFFLES:

1⅓ cups unbleached all-purpose flour

3 tablespoons whole wheat flour

2 teaspoons baking soda

⅓ cup plus 3 tablespoons granulated sugar, divided

¾ teaspoon kosher salt

½ cup pecan halves and pieces, toasted and finely chopped

2 large eggs, separated

1½ cups low-fat buttermilk

¼ cup (½ stick) unsalted butter, melted

FOR THE ROASTED BANANAS:

4 medium bananas, cut into ½-inch coins

2 tablespoons pure maple syrup

¼ cup packed light brown sugar

½ teaspoon ground cinnamon

2 tablespoons unsalted butter

FOR THE VANILLA WHIPPED CREAM:

1 cup heavy cream

2 teaspoons pure vanilla extract

Vegetable oil spray

7. Preheat a waffle iron and spray it with the vegetable oil. Ladle the waffle batter onto the iron and cook according to manufacturer's instructions. When the waffle is deep golden brown and crispy, transfer it to a plate and hold it in the warm oven. Repeat with the remaining batter.

8. To serve, top the waffles with the roasted bananas and a generous dollop of the whipped cream.

RESOURCES

Bob's Red Mill
www.bobsredmill.com
5000 SE International Wy
Milwaukie, OR 97222
800-349-2173
Great for alternative flours such as gluten-free corn flour, brown rice flour, tapioca flour, and xanthan gum

Chukar Cherries
www.chuckar.com
320 Wine Country Rd
Prosser, WA 99350
800-624-9544
Tart dried cherries, perfect for baking

Cupcake liners and wrappers
www.cupcakelinerswrappers.com
www.cupcakeswirl.com
Decorative cupcake wrappers that elevate a simple cupcake to a special dessert

Fairhaven Organic Flour Mill
www.fairhavenflour.com
808 North Hill Blvd
Burlington, WA 98233
360-757-9947
100 percent organic–certified, fresh-milled, intact whole grain flours; Macrina favorites include: oat flour, rye flour, whole wheat flour, rice flour, and cornmeal

Lodge Cast Iron Cookware
www.lodgemfg.com
423-837-7181
Double Dutch ovens for baking bread

Mt. Townsend Creamery
www.mttownsendcreamery.com
338 Sherman St
Port Townsend, WA 98368
360-379-0895
Wonderful artisan cheeses; Macrina favorite: fromage blanc

Nueske's
www.nueskes.com
800-392-2266
Delicious Applewood smoked bacon and other slow-smoked meat delicacies

Shepherd's Grain
www.shepherdsgrain.com
Great all-purpose flour, sold under the Stone Buhr label in most grocery stores

INDEX

ABOUT THE AUTHOR

The idea for Macrina Bakery & Café existed long before it opened its doors. The seed was planted while LESLIE MACKIE was in cooking school and continued to take root throughout her early restaurant career and during her travels. Mackie picked up her kitchen skills at the California Culinary Academy in San Francisco, but baking was her true love. She was among the first wave of Americans experimenting with recipes from European master bakers and a long, slow fermentation process. Mackie rediscovered the craft's traditional, almost spiritual importance. "To me, making bread is being an artist," Mackie says. "In France, bakers are revered because bread is such a central part of the family and the community."

Leslie was head baker at Seattle's Grand Central Bakery; then in 1993 opened her own place, Macrina. The Café & Bakery has been written up in *Sunset*, *Pacific Magazine*, *Bon Appetit*, *The LA Times* and *The New York Times*, not to mention endless coverage and accolades in *The Seattle Times*, *Seattle Weekly*, *Seattle* magazine, and *Seattle Met* magazine. Leslie's recipes reach well beyond Seattle, from her appearances on Julia Child's *Baking with Julia* television series (and inclusion in the companion cookbook) to features on many Food Network shows. Leslie has also received several nominations for the Outstanding Pastry Chef award from the James Beard Foundation, which honors food and beverage industry professionals in America for their achievements. They are the nation's most prestigious honors for culinary professionals.